SCHOLASTIC

Reproducible Forms
for the Writing Traits
Classroom
Middle School

RUTH CULHAM

New York • Toronto • London • Auckland • Sydney
Mexico City • New Delhi • Hong Kong • Buenos Aires

Teaching
Resources

Dedication

To the teachers, administrators, and school board of the Blue Springs School District in Blue Springs, Missouri, because you care so deeply about the writing lives of your students—which may be the greatest trait of all.

Editor: Raymond Coutu
Cover and Interior Designer: Maria Lilja
Copy Editor: Eileen Judge

ISBN-10: 0-545-13844-2
ISBN-13: 978-0-545-13844-4
Copyright © 2010 by Ruth Culham.
All rights reserved. Printed in the U.S.A.

2 3 4 5 6 7 8 9 10 40 14 13 12 11 10

Contents

Introduction

If you had one wish as a middle school writing teacher, what would it be? To have students who love to write? To have a steady stream of ideas to engage and motivate your students? To have new resources that help you make the best use of your teaching time? Of course! Picking only one of these wishes is tough, I'm sure, because together they are essential to a successful, dynamic writing classroom.

For students to write well and come to love writing, they need inspiration for coming up with writing topics, techniques for solving writing dilemmas, and time for making their pieces as strong as possible. Although implementing the strategies necessary to help students reach those goals may be a struggle, what matters most is that you, their teacher, actively support them in their efforts every single day.

Unfortunately, I can't snap my fingers and make your wishes come true. I can, however, provide you with trait-focused resources that will help you teach writing effectively and efficiently, and make your job more satisfying on a day-to-day basis. I can give you scoring guides, scoring sheets, and record-keeping forms to capture and chronicle your students' progress. I can give you question lists and feedback forms to guide conference conversations. I can give you printable tools for your students—charts, checklists, and self-assessment forms. I can even give you letter templates that teach parents how to support their children's writing at home. You'll find these and many other ready-to-use forms in this book—over 50 forms that may not make all your wishes come true, but can make teaching writing at the middle school level easier and more enjoyable for you and your students.

The book is divided into two sections, one for teachers and the other for students, with clear guidelines on how and when to use each form, whether it be with individual students, small groups, or the whole class.

Forms for teachers include:

* New 6-point, trait-specific scoring guides just for middle school teachers

* One-page scoring guides based on 4-, 5-, and 6-point scales

* Record-keeping forms to track how individual students are progressing and how the whole class has performed on a specific writing assignment

* Scoring guides for each writing mode: narrative, expository, and persuasive

* Student feedback forms for each mode

* Forms for planning lessons and conferences

* Teacher-to-home letters

Forms for students include:

* Take-home letters on the traits and the modes

* Forms that help students draft, revise, and edit their work

* Handy lists of key qualities for each trait and "Think About" questions for each key quality

* Peer conference guides

* A chart of editor's marks

* Student-friendly, trait-specific scoring guides

* Student publishing checklists

* Self-evaluation and reflection forms

All forms are presented as full-size blackline masters, making photocopying a breeze. You'll also find them on the accompanying CD, which enables you to print them from your computer or display them for the whole class, using an electronic projection system. *Reproducible Forms for the Writing Traits Classroom: Middle School* can be used on its own or as the ideal companion to my book *Traits of Writing: The Complete Guide for Middle School* (Scholastic, 2010).

Some Background on the Traits of Writing

The traits of writing provide the language we use to describe what writers really do as they draft, revise, and edit. As such, we can use them to drive assessment, instruction, and classroom talk.

Ideas: The piece's content—its central message and details that support that message.

Organization: The internal structure of the piece—the thread of logic, the pattern of meaning.

Voice: The tone and tenor of the piece—the personal stamp of the writer, which is achieved through a strong understanding of purpose and audience.

Word Choice: The specific vocabulary the writer uses to convey meaning and enlighten the reader.

Sentence Fluency: The way words and phrases flow through the piece. It is the auditory trait because it's "read" with the ear as much as the eye.

Conventions: The mechanical correctness of the piece. Correct use of conventions (spelling, capitalization, punctuation, paragraphing, and grammar and usage) guides the reader through the text easily.

Presentation: The physical appearance of the piece. A visually appealing text provides a welcome mat. It invites the reader in.

Assessment

Using the scoring guides and scoring sheets on pages 12–22, you can assess a piece of writing for one or more traits to identify what the student is doing well and what he or she needs work on through revision or editing. The scoring guides might reveal that the student needs to refocus the topic (ideas); think of a different way to introduce the piece (organization); reconsider the match between the piece's tone and its audience (voice); fine-tune the language to be more specific and accurate (word choice); smooth out awkward-sounding spots (sentence fluency); edit for spelling, capitalization, punctuation, paragraphing, or grammar and usage (conventions); and/or polish the piece to give it a finished appearance (presentation).

Instruction

Once you've assessed the papers of all your students and have identified areas of strength and weakness, you can use the scores to determine the most appropriate targets for instruction. For example, if many of the students in the class score a 1 or 2 in organization, you would plan to teach and reinforce key qualities of this trait in lessons and activities over the next few weeks. Teaching to areas of greatest need: That's how we use assessment data as the focus for instruction.

Classroom Talk

If you walk into a trait-based writing classroom, you will find students and teachers using the language of the traits as they engage in drafting, revising, and editing. Whether it is in a small group, large group, or one-on-one conference, the language of the traits provides a common framework for noting strong work and improving other pieces over time. Listen closely to the talk in a writing traits classroom to understand how much more helpful it is to offer focused feedback (rather than general, nonspecific comments).

> "Destiny, the way you described the rusty, old metal harness you found in your grandfather's barn helped me to understand more about how, as he has aged, he's had to give up favorite activities like horseback riding. When writers use thoughtful details like this, it makes the <u>idea</u> feel real and important to the reader."

> "What a great way to begin this piece, Cameron. I found myself intrigued about the changes in everyday life in Afghanistan because, in the lead of your essay, you provided such a vivid description of what I might see if I went there. The <u>organization</u> of your piece starts out strong with this introduction."

> "It felt like you were speaking right to me about the critical need to fund local animal shelters, Tony. Your examples, the passion you have for this topic, and how clearly you understood what I'd need to know to grasp the key issues on this topic come through loud and clear— that's your <u>voice</u>. And it's powerful in this piece."

> "'Whoosh!' 'Zap.' 'Shazam.' Your use of onomatopoeia gives a soundtrack to your writing, Carlos. I could hear it as I read. Spending time <u>choosing</u> the 'just-right' <u>words</u> and phrases makes your piece memorable and delightful to read."

> "Your essay on weather phenomena reads smoothly—especially in the third paragraph, Jane. I appreciate how you've varied the <u>sentences</u> in length and structure to provide <u>fluency</u> so I was able to get caught up in the sound of the writing along with your ideas at this critical part of the piece."

"Thank you, Jem, for taking the time to go back over your writing and edit it carefully for spelling, punctuation, and capitalization. It makes it so much easier for me to read your piece when it's this cleanly edited. Look for one place in the last paragraph where the subject-verb agreement is not aligned. Other than that, nice work with <u>conventions</u>."

Some Background on the Modes of Writing

While the traits help writers develop their work according to common characteristics of writing, the modes help them establish and maintain a purpose for writing.

Narrative: to tell a story

Expository: to inform or explain

Persuasive: to construct an argument

During prewriting and early drafting, writers tend to focus on mode. They decide whether they are going to tell a story to the reader, explain something to the reader, or try to convince the reader of something. As the writer takes the piece through the writing process, he or she may blend modes to create the strongest pieces possible: a narrative piece may contain an explanation to help the story unfold; an expository piece might contain a story to bring out a key point; a persuasive piece might contain both narrative and expository elements to build the strongest case possible.

The writer's choice of mode influences how he or she applies each of the traits. A narrative piece, for example, is organized quite differently than an expository piece. The voice of a persuasive piece is likely to be more strident than the voice of a narrative piece, which is likely to be more entertaining. Consider this assignment: "Write about a teacher who made a strong impression on you as a learner." An essay that explains the specific reasons the teacher stands out in the writer's memory (expository) is probably going to be quite different from a story about a typical day in the teacher's class (narrative). And if the writer chooses to create a plea for all teachers to have the same positive qualities as the teacher he or she identifies for the assignment (persuasive), it would be written differently from a narrative or expository piece. As students write, it's important for them to keep the purpose (mode) of their writing clearly in mind and apply the traits appropriately.

Although traits and modes can be taught individually, students make greater strides when they are taught in unison. Unleashing the power of the traits and modes simultaneously inspires students to create strong, powerful pieces of writing. The mode scoring guides on pages 23–25 help you and your students look at traits and modes through a single lens.

Concluding Thoughts

Planning instruction, assessing student work, organizing instructional materials, providing quick and effective feedback, and keeping accurate records are a big part of a writing teacher's daily reality. It's not easy to handle all these teaching activities simultaneously, however. The forms in this book are designed to give you a helping hand as you guide your middle school students in becoming strong writers.

SECTION I

Reproducible Forms for Teachers

In this section, you'll find three sets of forms to help you assess writing, confer with students, keep records, plan instruction, and communicate with family members. The forms are organized according to the following categories:

* Assessment Tools and Feedback Forms

* Record-Keeping and Planning Forms

* Home Communication Forms

This expansive collection of forms represents an exciting breakthrough for middle school teachers. You'll appreciate how easy the new trait-specific scoring guides are to use to assess writing and create a yearlong framework for writing instruction. And there are mode-specific scoring guides, too, which help you teach students about the specific purposes for writing: to tell a story (narrative), to inform or explain (expository), and to construct an argument (persuasive). The trait- and mode-specific scoring guides will surely take your writing instruction to new heights, as will all the other forms in this section.

Assessment Tools and Feedback Forms

For assessment to be instructive, it must provide information that can be used to plan teaching. It must reveal strengths in student writing as well as areas of need that, in turn, can be specifically addressed in classroom lessons and activities. That means the assessment criteria must capture what good writing looks like and provide teachers and students with a clear target for success in writing. After all, when we have a focused picture of where we're going, it's easier to get there. Scoring guides for the traits and the modes are included in this section, along with record-keeping forms to document results, and feedback forms to guide students in revision and editing.

Trait-Specific Scoring Guides

Use the seven full-page, trait-specific scoring guides to assess writing performance trait by trait, in detail, on a 6-point scale that ranges from rudimentary to exceptional. They can be used to assess for one or more traits, depending on the circumstance of the assessment. These scoring guides are new, specially designed to address the writing of middle school students.

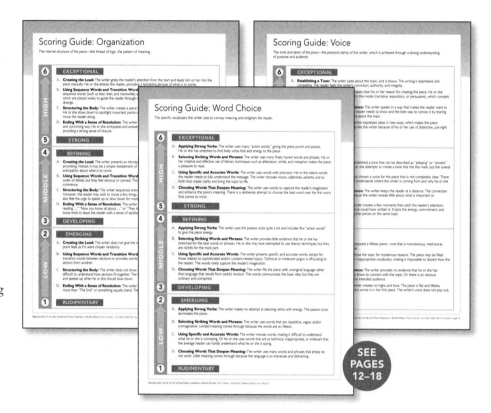

SEE
PAGES
12–18

One-Page, Teacher-Friendly Scoring Guides

These three scoring guides cover all seven traits on a single page. Though not as detailed as the full-page, trait-specific scoring guides, they allow you to check student work quickly for baseline information, based on a 4-, 5-, or 6-point scale. They give you a quick glimpse at the traits. Use the guide that matches the scale you prefer.

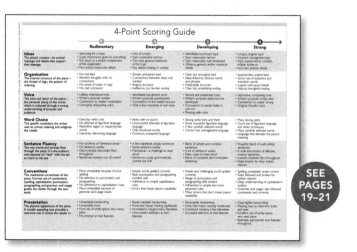

SEE
PAGES
19–21

Cut-Apart Scoring Sheets

The scoring sheets provide a handy way to deliver assessment feedback to students. They can be used for one trait, all seven traits, or any number in between. I've included 4-, 5-, and 6-point versions that correspond to the scoring guide you use to conduct the assessment.

SEE PAGE 22

Modes of Writing Scoring Guides

Use the mode-specific scoring guides for narrative, expository, and persuasive writing to determine how well a student's purpose for writing is being communicated to the reader. These guides are based on a 6-point scale and help you provide information to students about their writing, above and beyond the traits.

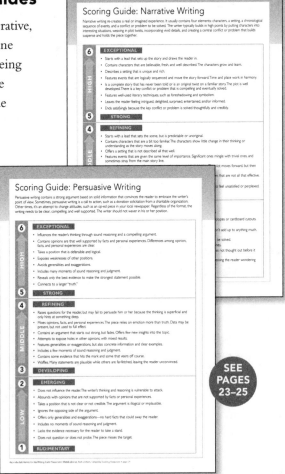

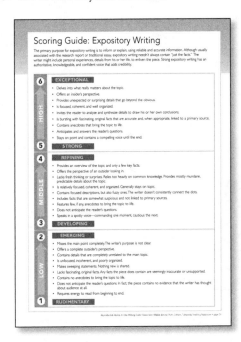

SEE PAGES 23–25

Student Feedback Forms

The student feedback forms allow you to respond to student work by focusing on one trait at a time. By identifying where the work falls on the form's continuum, you show the student how close he or she is to making the work as clear and strong as possible. There's also space for making quick suggestions for revising and editing. Students can also use these forms on their own, in peer conferences.

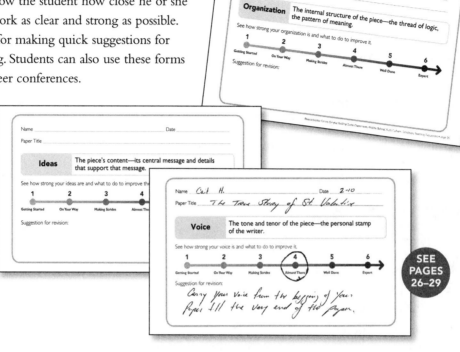

Ready-to-Publish Checklist

This is a versatile checklist that can be used in its entirety to provide feedback on all traits or in sections for selected traits. Use it to discuss how a piece is developing, noting the traits of which the student has a firm grasp and those that could use attention, as he or she prepares a final copy.

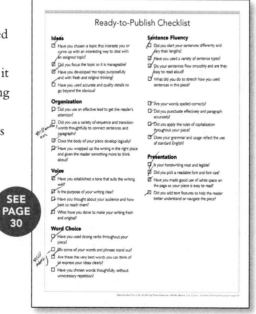

Scoring Guide: Ideas

The piece's content—its central message and details that support that message.

6 EXCEPTIONAL

HIGH

A. **Finding a Topic:** The writer offers a clear, central theme or a simple, original story line that is memorable.

B. **Focusing the Topic:** The writer narrows the theme or story line to create a piece that is clear, tight, and manageable.

C. **Developing the Topic:** The writer provides enough critical evidence to support the theme and shows insight on the topic. Or he or she tells the story in a fresh way through an original, unpredictable plot.

D. **Using Details:** The writer offers credible, accurate details that create pictures in the reader's mind, from the beginning of the piece to the end. Those details provide the reader with evidence of the writer's knowledge about and/or experience with the topic.

5 STRONG

4 REFINING

MIDDLE

A. **Finding a Topic:** The writer offers a recognizable but broad theme or story line. He or she stays on topic, but in a predictable way.

B. **Focusing the Topic:** The writer needs to crystallize his or her topic around the central theme or story line. He or she does not focus on a specific aspect of the topic.

C. **Developing the Topic:** The writer draws on personal knowledge and experience, but does not offer a unique perspective. He or she does not probe deeply, but instead gives the reader only a glimpse at aspects of the topic.

D. **Using Details:** The writer offers details, but they do not always hit the mark because they are inaccurate or irrelevant. He or she does not create a picture in the reader's mind because key questions about the central theme or story line have not been addressed.

3 DEVELOPING

2 EMERGING

LOW

A. **Finding a Topic:** The writer has not settled on a topic and, therefore, may offer only a series of unfocused, repetitious, and/or random thoughts.

B. **Focusing the Topic:** The writer has not narrowed his or her topic in a meaningful way. It's hard to tell what the writer thinks is important since he or she devotes equal importance to each piece of information.

C. **Developing the Topic:** The writer has created a piece that is so short the reader cannot fully understand or appreciate what he or she wants to say. He or she may have simply restated an assigned topic or responded to a prompt without devoting much thought or effort to it.

D. **Using Details:** The writer has clearly devoted little attention to details. The writing contains limited or completely inaccurate information. After reading the piece, the reader is left with many unanswered questions.

1 RUDIMENTARY

Scoring Guide: Organization

The internal structure of the piece—the thread of logic, the pattern of meaning.

6 — HIGH

EXCEPTIONAL

A. **Creating the Lead:** The writer grabs the reader's attention from the start and leads him or her into the piece naturally. He or she entices the reader, providing a tantalizing glimpse of what is to come.

B. **Using Sequence Words and Transition Words:** The writer includes a variety of carefully selected sequence words (such as *later*, *then*, and *meanwhile*) and transition words (such as *however*, *also*, and *clearly*), which are placed wisely to guide the reader through the piece by showing how ideas progress, relate, and/or diverge.

C. **Structuring the Body:** The writer creates a piece that is easy to follow by fitting details together logically. He or she slows down to spotlight important points or events, and speeds up when he or she needs to move the reader along.

D. **Ending With a Sense of Resolution:** The writer sums up his or her thinking in a natural, thoughtful, and convincing way. He or she anticipates and answers any lingering questions the reader may have, providing a strong sense of closure.

5

STRONG

4 — MIDDLE

REFINING

A. **Creating the Lead:** The writer presents an introduction, although it may not be original or thought-provoking. Instead, it may be a simple restatement of the topic and, therefore, does not create a sense of anticipation about what is to come.

B. **Using Sequence Words and Transition Words:** The writer uses sequence words to show the logical order of details, but they feel obvious or canned. The use of transition words is spotty and rarely creates coherence.

C. **Structuring the Body:** The writer sequences events and important points logically, for the most part. However, the reader may wish to move a few things around to create a more sensible flow. He or she may also feel the urge to speed up or slow down for more satisfying pacing.

D. **Ending With a Sense of Resolution:** The writer ends the piece on a familiar note: "Thank you for reading…," "Now you know all about…," or "They lived happily ever after." He or she needs to tie up loose ends to leave the reader with a sense of satisfaction or closure.

3

DEVELOPING

2 — LOW

EMERGING

A. **Creating the Lead:** The writer does not give the reader any clue about what is to come. The opening point feels as if it were chosen randomly.

B. **Using Sequence Words and Transition Words:** The writer does not provide sequence and/or transition words between sections or provides words that are so confusing the reader is unable to sort one section from another.

C. **Structuring the Body:** The writer does not show clearly what comes first, next, and last, making it difficult to understand how sections fit together. The writer slows down when he or she should speed up, and speeds up when he or she should slow down.

D. **Ending With a Sense of Resolution:** The writer ends the piece with no conclusion at all—or nothing more than "The End" or something equally bland. There is no sense of resolution, no sense of completion.

1

RUDIMENTARY

Scoring Guide: Voice

The tone and tenor of the piece—the personal stamp of the writer, which is achieved through a strong understanding of purpose and audience.

6

HIGH

EXCEPTIONAL

A. **Establishing a Tone:** The writer cares about the topic, and it shows. The writing is expressive and compelling. The reader feels the writer's conviction, authority, and integrity.

B. **Conveying the Purpose:** The writer makes clear his or her reason for creating the piece. He or she offers a point of view that is appropriate for the mode (narrative, expository, or persuasive), which compels the reader to read on.

C. **Creating a Connection to the Audience:** The writer speaks in a way that makes the reader want to listen. He or she has considered what the reader needs to know and the best way to convey it by sharing his or her fascination, feelings, and opinions about the topic.

D. **Taking Risks to Create Voice:** The writer expresses ideas in new ways, which makes the piece interesting and original. The writing sounds like the writer because of his or her use of distinctive, just-right words and phrases.

5

STRONG

4

MIDDLE

REFINING

A. **Establishing a Tone:** The writer has established a tone that can be described as "pleasing" or "sincere," but not "passionate" or "compelling." He or she attempts to create a tone that hits the mark, but the overall result feels generic.

B. **Conveying the Purpose:** The writer has chosen a voice for the piece that is not completely clear. There are only a few moments when the reader understands where the writer is coming from and why he or she wrote the piece.

C. **Creating a Connection to the Audience:** The writer keeps the reader at a distance. The connection between reader and writer is tenuous because the writer reveals little about what is important or meaningful about the topic.

D. **Taking Risks to Create Voice:** The writer creates a few moments that catch the reader's attention, but only a few. The piece sounds like anyone could have written it. It lacks the energy, commitment, and conviction that would distinguish it from other pieces on the same topic.

3

DEVELOPING

2

LOW

EMERGING

A. **Establishing a Tone:** The writer has produced a lifeless piece—one that is monotonous, mechanical, repetitious, and/or off-putting to the reader.

B. **Conveying the Purpose:** The writer chose the topic for mysterious reasons. The piece may be filled with random thoughts, technical jargon, or inappropriate vocabulary, making it impossible to discern how the writer feels about the topic.

C. **Creating a Connection to the Audience:** The writer provides no evidence that he or she has considered what the reader might need to know to connect with the topic. Or there is an obvious mismatch between the piece's tone and the intended audience.

D. **Taking Risks to Create Voice:** The writer creates no highs and lows. The piece is flat and lifeless, causing the reader to wonder why he or she wrote it in the first place. The writer's voice does not pop out, even for a moment.

1

RUDIMENTARY

Scoring Guide: Word Choice

The specific vocabulary the writer uses to convey meaning and enlighten the reader.

6 EXCEPTIONAL

HIGH

A. Applying Strong Verbs: The writer uses many "action words," giving the piece punch and pizzazz. He or she has stretched to find lively verbs that add energy to the piece.

B. Selecting Striking Words and Phrases: The writer uses many finely honed words and phrases. His or her creative and effective use of literary techniques such as alliteration, simile, and metaphor makes the piece a pleasure to read.

C. Using Specific and Accurate Words: The writer uses words with precision. He or she selects words the reader needs to fully understand the message. The writer chooses nouns, adjectives, adverbs, and so forth that create clarity and bring the topic to life.

D. Choosing Words That Deepen Meaning: The writer uses words to capture the reader's imagination and enhance the piece's meaning. There is a deliberate attempt to choose the best word over the first word that comes to mind.

5 STRONG

4 REFINING

MIDDLE

A. Applying Strong Verbs: The writer uses the passive voice quite a bit and includes few "action words" to give the piece energy.

B. Selecting Striking Words and Phrases: The writer provides little evidence that he or she has stretched for the best words or phrases. He or she may have attempted to use literary techniques, but they are clichés for the most part.

C. Using Specific and Accurate Words: The writer presents specific and accurate words, except for those related to sophisticated and/or content-related topics. Technical or irrelevant jargon is off-putting to the reader. The words rarely capture the reader's imagination.

D. Choosing Words That Deepen Meaning: The writer fills the piece with unoriginal language rather than language that results from careful revision. The words communicate the basic idea, but they are ordinary and uninspired.

3 DEVELOPING

2 EMERGING

LOW

A. Applying Strong Verbs: The writer makes no attempt at selecting verbs with energy. The passive voice dominates the piece.

B. Selecting Striking Words and Phrases: The writer uses words that are repetitive, vague, and/or unimaginative. Limited meaning comes through because the words are so lifeless.

C. Using Specific and Accurate Words: The writer misuses words, making it difficult to understand what what he or she is attempting to convey. Or he or she uses words that are so technical, inappropriate, or irrelevant that the average reader can hardly understand what he or she is saying.

D. Choosing Words That Deepen Meaning: The writer uses many words and phrases that simply do not work. Little meaning comes through because the language is so imprecise and distracting.

1 RUDIMENTARY

Scoring Guide: Sentence Fluency

The way words and phrases flow through the piece. It is the auditory trait because it's "read" with the ear as much as the eye.

6 **HIGH**

EXCEPTIONAL

A. **Crafting Well-Built Sentences:** The writer carefully and creatively constructs sentences for maximum impact. Transition words such as *but*, *and*, and *so* are used successfully to join sentences and sentence parts.

B. **Varying Sentence Types:** The writer uses various types of sentences (simple, compound, and/or complex) to enhance the central theme or story line. The piece is made up of an effective mix of long, complex sentences and short, simple ones.

C. **Capturing Smooth and Rhythmic Flow:** The writer thinks about how the sentences sound. He or she uses phrasing that is almost musical. If the piece were read aloud, it would be easy on the ear.

D. **Breaking the "Rules" to Create Fluency:** The writer diverges from standard English to create interest and impact. For example, he or she may use a sentence fragment, such as "All alone in the forest," or a single word, such as "Bam!" to accent a particular moment or action. He or she might begin with informal words such as *well*, *and*, or *but* to create a conversational tone, or he or she might break rules intentionally to make dialogue sound authentic.

5 ### STRONG

4 **MIDDLE**

REFINING

A. **Crafting Well-Built Sentences:** The writer offers simple sentences that are sound but no long, complex ones. He or she attempts to vary the beginnings and lengths of sentences.

B. **Varying Sentence Types:** The writer exhibits basic sentence sense and offers some sentence variety. He or she attempts to use different types of sentences, but in doing so creates an uneven flow rather than a smooth, seamless one.

C. **Capturing Smooth and Rhythmic Flow:** The writer has produced a text that is uneven. Many sentences read smoothly, whereas others are choppy or awkward.

D. **Breaking the "Rules" to Create Fluency:** The writer includes fragments, but they seem more accidental than intentional. He or she uses informal words such as *well*, *and*, and *but* inappropriately to start sentences, and pays little attention to making dialogue sound authentic.

3 ### DEVELOPING

2 **LOW**

EMERGING

A. **Crafting Well-Built Sentences:** The writer's sentences, even simple ones, are often flawed. Sentence beginnings are repetitive and uninspired.

B. **Varying Sentence Types:** The writer uses a single, repetitive sentence pattern throughout or connects sentence parts with an endless string of transition words such as *and*, *but*, *or*, and *because*, which distracts the reader.

C. **Capturing Smooth and Rhythmic Flow:** The writer has created a text that is a challenge to read aloud since the sentences are incomplete, choppy, stilted, rambling, and/or awkward.

D. **Breaking the "Rules" to Create Fluency:** The writer offers few or no simple, well-built sentences, making it impossible to determine whether he or she has done anything out of the ordinary. Global revision is necessary before sentences can be revised for stylistic and creative purposes.

1 ### RUDIMENTARY

Scoring Guide: Conventions

The mechanical correctness of the piece. Correct use of conventions (spelling, capitalization, punctuation, paragraphing, and grammar and usage) guides the reader through the text easily.

HIGH

6

EXCEPTIONAL

A. **Checking Spelling:** The writer spells sight words, high-frequency words, and less familiar words correctly. When he or she spells less familiar words incorrectly, those words are phonetically correct. Overall, the piece reveals control in spelling.

B. **Punctuating Effectively and Paragraphing Accurately:** The writer handles basic punctuation skillfully. He or she understands how to use periods, commas, question marks, and exclamation points to enhance clarity and meaning. Paragraphs are indented in the right places. The piece is ready for a general audience.

C. **Capitalizing Correctly:** The writer uses capital letters consistently and accurately. A deep understanding of how to capitalize dialogue, abbreviations, proper names, and titles is evident.

D. **Applying Grammar and Usage:** The writer forms grammatically correct phrases and sentences. He or she shows care in applying the rules of standard English. The writer may break from those rules for stylistic reasons, but otherwise abides by them.

5

STRONG

MIDDLE

4

REFINING

A. **Checking Spelling:** The writer incorrectly spells a few high-frequency words and many unfamiliar words and/or sophisticated words.

B. **Punctuating Effectively and Paragraphing Accurately:** The writer handles basic punctuation marks (such as end marks on sentences and commas in a series) well. However, he or she might have trouble with more complex punctuation marks (such as quotation marks, parentheses, and dashes) and with paragraphing, especially on longer pieces.

C. **Capitalizing Correctly:** The writer capitalizes the first word in sentences and most common proper nouns. However, his or her use of more complex capitalization is spotty when it comes to dialogue, abbreviations, and proper names ("*aunt Maria*" instead of "*Aunt Maria*" or "*my aunt*," for instance).

D. **Applying Grammar and Usage:** The writer has made grammar and usage mistakes throughout the piece, but they do not interfere with the reader's ability to understand the message. Issues related to agreement, tense, and word usage appear here and there, but can be easily corrected.

3

DEVELOPING

LOW

2

EMERGING

A. **Checking Spelling:** The writer has misspelled many words, even simple ones, which causes the reader to focus on conventions rather than on the central theme or story line.

B. **Punctuating Effectively and Paragraphing Accurately:** The writer has neglected to use punctuation, used punctuation incorrectly, and/or forgotten to indent paragraphs, making it difficult for the reader to find meaning.

C. **Capitalizing Correctly:** The writer uses capitals inconsistently, even in common places such as the first word in the sentence. He or she uses capitals correctly in some places but has no consistent control over them.

D. **Applying Grammar and Usage:** The writer makes frequent mistakes in grammar and usage, making it difficult to read and understand the piece. Issues related to agreement, tense, and word usage abound.

1

RUDIMENTARY

Scoring Guide: Presentation

The physical appearance of the piece. A visually appealing text provides a welcome mat. It invites the reader in.

6 — HIGH

EXCEPTIONAL

A. Applying Handwriting Skills: The writer uses handwriting that is clear and legible. Whether he or she prints or uses cursive, letters are uniform and slant evenly throughout the piece. Spacing between words is consistent.

B. Using Word Processing Effectively: The writer uses a font style and size that are easy to read and are a good match for the piece's purpose. If he or she uses color, it enhances the piece's readability.

C. Making Good Use of White Space: The writer frames the text with appropriately sized margins. Artful spacing between letters, words, and lines makes reading a breeze. There are no cross-outs, smudges, or tears on the paper.

D. Refining Text Features: The writer effectively places text features such as headings, page numbers, titles, and bullets on the page and aligns them clearly with the text they support.

5

STRONG

4 — MIDDLE

REFINING

A. Applying Handwriting Skills: The writer has readable handwriting, but his or her inconsistent letter slanting, spacing, and formation distract from the central theme or story line.

B. Using Word Processing Effectively: The writer uses an easy-to-read font but formats it in a way that makes the piece cluttered and distracting. His or her choice of font style and/or size may not match the writing's purpose. He or she may use color with varying degrees of success.

C. Making Good Use of White Space: The writer creates margins but they are inconsistent or ineffective as a frame for the piece. Spacing between letters, words, and lines makes reading difficult at times. An occasional cross-out or smudge blemishes the piece.

D. Refining Text Features: The writer includes complex text features such as charts, graphs, maps, and tables, but not clearly or consistently. However, he or she does a good job with less complex features such as the size and placement of the title, bullets, sidebars, subheadings, illustrations, and page numbers.

3

DEVELOPING

2 — LOW

EMERGING

A. Applying Handwriting Skills: The writer forms letters and uses space in a way that makes the piece virtually illegible. The handwriting is a visual barrier.

B. Using Word Processing Effectively: The writer creates a dizzying display of different font styles and sizes, making the piece virtually unreadable. The misuse of color also detracts.

C. Making Good Use of White Space: The writer formats margins inconsistently and uses white space ineffectively, making the piece hard to read. Space between letters, words, and lines is nonexistent, or there is so much space it's distracting.

D. Refining Text Features: The writer does not include features or includes features that are confusing or indecipherable rather than useful to the reader. The paper is seriously marred with cross-outs, smudges, and/or tears.

1

RUDIMENTARY

4-Point Scoring Guide

Trait	Rudimentary (1)	Emerging (2)	Developing (3)	Strong (4)
Ideas The piece's content—its central message and details that support that message.	• Searching for a topic • Equal importance given to everything • Too short or a simple restatement of the assignment • Few and/or inaccurate details	• Hint of a topic • Topic somewhat narrow • The most general treatment of the topic • Key details missing or unclear	• Identifiable but broad topic • Topic reasonably narrow • Topic reasonably well developed • Obvious, general, and/or imprecise details	• Unique, original topic • Focused, manageable topic • Topic supported by credible, reliable evidence • Accurate, precise details
Organization The internal structure of the piece—the thread of logic, the pattern of meaning.	• No real lead • Random thoughts with no connections • No sense of order or logic • No real conclusion	• Simple, uninspired lead • Connections between ideas only implied • Illogical structure • Ineffective, too familiar ending	• Clear but unoriginal lead • Ideas linked by obvious words and phrases • Predictable structure • Clear but unsatisfying ending	• Appropriate, original lead • Good use of sequence and transition words • Logical, well-paced details • Natural, thoughtful ending
Voice The tone and tenor of the piece—the personal stamp of the writer, which is achieved through a strong understanding of purpose and audience.	• Lifeless, mechanical tone • Writer's purpose unclear • Connection to reader nonexistent • Unoriginal, uninspiring voice	• Identifiable but generic tone • Writer's purpose questionable • Connection to the reader tenuous • Only a few moments of real voice	• Sincere but passionless tone • Writer's purpose stated but not developed • Connection to reader fades in and out • Pleasing, safe voice	• Expressive, compelling tone • Writer's purpose crystal clear • Connection to reader strong • Original, forceful voice
Word Choice The specific vocabulary the writer uses to convey meaning and enlighten the reader.	• Everyday verbs only • No attempt at figurative language • Repetitive, vague, or inappropriate words • Imprecise, distracting language	• Verbs with no punch • Unsuccessful attempts at figurative language • Only functional words • Common, uninspired language	• Strong verbs here and there • Some successful figurative language • A few carefully selected words • Correct but unimaginative language	• Many strong verbs • Good use of figurative language and other techniques • Many carefully selected words • Language that elevates the piece's meaning
Sentence Fluency The way words and phrases flow through the piece. It is the auditory trait because it's "read" with the ear as much as the eye.	• No evidence of "sentence sense" • No sentence variety • Disconnected, discordant flow throughout • Sentences random, out of control	• A few repetitive, simple sentences • Some sentence variety • Mechanical—a challenge to read aloud • Sentences usually grammatically correct but dull	• Blend of simple and complex sentences • A lot of sentence variety • Fluid—easy to read aloud • Blend of complete and incomplete sentences	• Powerful blend of well-crafted sentences • A solid assortment of effective, creative sentences • Smooth, rhythmic flow throughout • Rules broken for clear stylistic reasons
Conventions The mechanical correctness of the piece. Correct use of conventions (spelling, capitalization, punctuation, paragraphing, and grammar and usage) guides the reader through the text easily.	• Piece unreadable because of poor spelling • No attention to punctuation and paragraphing • No adherence to capitalization rules • Piece unreadable because of grammar and usage issues	• Simple words spelled correctly • Basic punctuation and paragraphing handled well • Adherence to simple capitalization rules • Errors that impair piece's readability	• Simple and challenging words spelled correctly • Range of punctuation and paragraphing skills evident • Adherence to simple and more advanced rules • Minor errors that don't impair piece's readability	• Spelling completely under control • Rules followed and broken for stylistic reasons • Deep understanding of capitalization evident • Grammar and usage rules followed consistently and correctly
Presentation The physical appearance of the piece. A visually appealing text provides a welcome mat. It invites the reader in.	• Unreadable handwriting • Unreadable fonts • Poor use of white space; very messy piece • No attempt at text features	• Barely readable handwriting • Fonts that impair reading significantly • Inconsistent margins; many blemishes • Unsuccessful attempts at text features	• Serviceable handwriting • Fonts that impair reading moderately • Consistent margins; a few blemishes • Successful attempts at text features	• Clear, legible handwriting • Pleasing, easy-to-read font styles and sizes • Excellent use of white space; very neat piece • Seamless, appropriate text features throughout

5-Point Scoring Guide

→

	1 Rudimentary	2 Emerging	3 Developing	4 Refining	5 Strong
Ideas The piece's content—its central message and details that support that message.	• Searching for a topic • Equal importance given to everything • Too short or a simple restatement of the assignment • Few details and/or inaccurate details	• Hint of a topic • No focus on an aspect of the topic • The most general treatment of the topic • Key details missing or unclear	• Identifiable but broad topic • Topic somewhat narrow • Only a glimpse at what matters • General, imprecise details	• Clear but predictable topic • Topic reasonably narrow • Topic reasonably well developed • A few accurate, precise details	• Unique, original topic • Focused, manageable topic • Topic supported by credible, reliable evidence • Many accurate, precise details
Organization The internal structure of the piece—the thread of logic, the pattern of meaning.	• No lead • Random thoughts with no connections • No sense of order or logic • No real conclusion	• Purpose of lead unclear • Connections between ideas only implied • Illogical structure • Ineffective ending	• Predictable lead • Common sequence and transition words • Canned structure • Forced ending	• Clear lead • Good use of sequence and transition words • Reasonably well-paced details • Clear but unsatisfying ending	• Effective, appropriate lead • Excellent use of sequence and transition words • Logical, well-paced details • Natural, thoughtful ending
Voice The tone and tenor of the piece—the personal stamp of the writer, which is achieved through a strong understanding of purpose and audience.	• Lifeless, mechanical tone • Writer's purpose unclear • Connection to reader nonexistent • Unoriginal, uninspiring voice	• Identifiable but generic tone • Writer's purpose questionable • Connection to reader tenuous • Only a few moments of real voice	• Sincere but passionless tone • Writer's purpose undeveloped • Connection to reader fades in and out • Pleasing, safe voice	• Expressive, compelling tone at times • Writer's purpose clear • Connection to reader average • Original, forceful voice	• Expressive, compelling tone throughout • Writer's purpose drives voice • Connection to reader strong • Voice that meets writer's audience and purpose
Word Choice The specific vocabulary the writer uses to convey meaning and enlighten the reader.	• Everyday verbs only • No attempt at figurative language • Repetitive, vague, or inappropriate words • Imprecise, distracting language	• Verbs with no punch • Unsuccessful attempts at figurative language • Only functional words • Common, uninspired language	• Strong verbs here and there • Successful attempt at figurative language • A few carefully selected words • Correct but unimaginative language	• Many strong verbs • Some strong figurative language • Many carefully selected words • Exceptional language here and there	• Strong verbs throughout • Good use of figurative language and other techniques • Every word selected carefully • Language that elevates the piece's meaning
Sentence Fluency The way words and phrases flow through the piece. It is the auditory trait because it's "read" with the ear as much as the eye.	• No evidence of "sentence sense" • No sentence variety • Disconnected, discordant flow throughout • Sentences random, out of control	• A few repetitive, simple sentences • Little sentence variety • Mechanical—a challenge to read aloud • Sentences usually grammatically correct but dull	• Awkward blend of simple and complex sentences • Some sentence variety • Sentences more mechanical than fluid • Awkward blend of complete and incomplete sentences	• Pleasing blend of simple and complex sentences • A lot of sentence variety • Fluid—easy to read aloud • Rules broken for apparent stylistic reasons	• Powerful blend of well-crafted sentences • A solid assortment of effective, creative sentences • Smooth, rhythmic flow throughout • Rules broken for clear stylistic reasons
Conventions The mechanical correctness of the piece. Correct use of conventions (spelling, capitalization, punctuation, paragraphing, and grammar and usage) guides the reader through the text easily.	• Piece unreadable because of poor spelling • No attention to punctuation and paragraphing • No adherence to capitalization rules • Piece unreadable because of grammar and usage issues	• Simple words spelled correctly • Little attention to punctuation and paragraphing • Little adherence to capitalization rules • Piece almost unreadable because of grammar and usage issues	• Simple and challenging words spelled correctly • Basic punctuation and paragraphing handled well • Adherence to simple capitalization rules • Errors that don't impair the piece's readability	• Spelling generally under control • More advanced punctuation and paragraphing handled well • Adherence to simple as well as more advanced rules • Grammar and usage rules followed consistently and correctly	• Spelling completely under control • Rules followed and broken for stylistic reasons • Deep understanding of capitalization evident • Clear mastery of the rules of standard English
Presentation The physical appearance of the piece. A visually appealing text provides a welcome mat. It invites the reader in.	• Unreadable handwriting • Unreadable fonts • Poor use of white space; very messy piece • No attempts at text features	• Barely readable handwriting • Fonts that impair reading significantly • Very inconsistent margins and spacing; messy piece • Unsuccessful attempts at text features	• Serviceable handwriting • Fonts that impair reading moderately • Somewhat inconsistent margins and spacing; many blemishes • Moderately successful attempts at text features	• Clear, legible handwriting • Appropriate font styles and sizes • Consistent margins and spacing; a few blemishes • Successful attempts at text features	• Pleasing, easy-to-read handwriting • Pleasing, easy-to-read font styles and sizes • Excellent use of white space; very neat piece • Seamless, appropriate text features throughout

6-Point Scoring Guide

	1 Rudimentary	2 Emerging	3 Developing	4 Refining	5 Strong	6 Exceptional
Ideas The piece's content—its central message and details that support that message.	• Searching for a topic • Equal importance given to everything • Too short or a simple restatement of the assignment • Few details and/or inaccurate details	• Hint of a topic • No focus on an aspect of the topic • The most general treatment of the topic • Key details missing or unclear	• Identifiable but broad topic • Topic somewhat narrow • Only a glimpse at what matters • General, imprecise details	• Clear but predictable topic • Topic reasonably narrow • Topic reasonably well developed • A few accurate, precise details	• Clear topic • Focused, manageable topic • Topic supported by credible evidence • Many accurate, precise details	• Unique, original topic • Laser-sharp focus on the topic • Topic supported by credible, reliable evidence • "Just-right" details create insider's perspective
Organization The internal structure of the piece—the thread of logic, the pattern of meaning.	• No real lead • Random thoughts with no connections • No sense of order or logic • No real conclusion	• Purpose of lead unclear • Connections between ideas only implied • Illogical structure • Ineffective ending	• Predictable lead • Common sequence and transition words • Canned structure • Forced ending	• Clear lead • Original sequence and transition words • Reasonably well-paced details • Clear but unsatisfying ending	• Effective, appropriate lead • Effective structure • Well-paced details • Satisfying ending	• Enticing, strong lead • Artful use of sequence and transition words • Highly effective structure • Powerful ending
Voice The tone and tenor of the piece—the personal stamp of the writer, which is achieved through a strong understanding of purpose and audience.	• Lifeless, mechanical tone • Writer's purpose unclear • Connection to reader nonexistent • Unoriginal, uninspiring voice	• Identifiable but generic tone • Writer's purpose questionable • Connection to reader tenuous • Hint of real voice	• Sincere but passionless tone • Writer's purpose somewhat clear • Connection to reader fades in and out • Only a few moments of real voice	• Established but weak tone • Writer's purpose undeveloped • Connection to reader average • Pleasing, safe voice	• Expressive, compelling tone at times • Writer's purpose clear • Connection to reader strong • Original, forceful voice	• Expressive, compelling tone throughout • Writer's purpose drives voice • Connection to reader drives voice • Voice that meets writer's audience and purpose
Word Choice The specific vocabulary the writer uses to convey meaning and enlighten the reader.	• Everyday verbs only • No attempt at figurative language • Repetitive, vague, or inappropriate words • Imprecise, distracting language	• Verbs with no punch • Unsuccessful attempts at figurative language • Only functional words • Common, uninspired language	• Verbs with little punch • Successful attempt at figurative language • Occasional carefully selected words • Correct but uninspired language	• Strong verbs here and there • Some successful figurative language • A few carefully selected words • Good language here and there	• Many strong verbs • A lot of successful figurative language • Many carefully selected words • Exceptional language here and there	• Strong verbs throughout • Good use of figurative language and other techniques • Every word selected carefully • Language that elevates the piece's meaning
Sentence Fluency The way words and phrases flow through the piece. It is the auditory trait because it's "read" with the ear as much as the eye.	• No evidence of "sentence sense" • No sentence variety • Disconnected, discordant flow • Sentences random, out of control	• A few repetitive, simple sentences • Little sentence variety • Mechanical—a challenge to read aloud • Sentences usually grammatically correct but dull	• Awkward blend of simple and complex sentences • Some sentence variety • Sentences more mechanical than fluid • Awkward blend of complete and incomplete sentences	• Mediocre blend of simple and complex sentences • A lot of sentence variety • Sentences more fluid than mechanical • Smoother blend of complete and incomplete sentences	• Pleasing blend of simple and complex sentences • A solid assortment of effective sentences • Fluid—easy to read aloud • Rules broken for apparent stylistic reasons	• Powerful blend of well-crafted sentences • Fluency and meaning enhanced by sentence variety • Smooth, rhythmic flow throughout • Rules broken for clear stylistic reasons
Conventions The mechanical correctness of the piece. Correct use of conventions (spelling, capitalization, punctuation, paragraphing, and usage) guides the reader through the text easily.	• Piece unreadable because of poor spelling • No attention to punctuation and paragraphing • No adherence to capitalization rules • Piece unreadable because of grammar and usage issues	• Piece almost unreadable because of poor spelling • Little attention to punctuation and paragraphing • Little adherence to capitalization rules • Piece almost unreadable because of grammar and usage issues	• Simple words spelled correctly • Basic punctuation and paragraphing handled well • Adherence to simple capitalization rules • Errors that impair piece's readability	• Simple and challenging words spelled correctly • More advanced punctuation and paragraphing handled well • Adherence to simple as well as more advanced rules • Errors that don't impair piece's readability	• Spelling generally under control • Range of punctuation and paragraphing skills evident • Solid control over capitalization • Grammar and usage rules followed consistently and correctly	• Spelling completely under control • Rules followed and broken for stylistic reasons • Deep understanding of capitalization evident • Clear mastery of the rules of standard English
Presentation The physical appearance of the piece. A visually appealing text provides a welcome mat. It invites the reader in.	• Unreadable handwriting • Unreadable fonts • Poor use of white space; very messy piece • No attempt at text features	• Barely readable handwriting throughout • Fonts that impair reading significantly • Very inconsistent margins and spacing; messy piece • Unsuccessful attempts at text features	• Handwriting that begins well but ends poorly • Cluttered font styles and sizes • Somewhat inconsistent margins; many blemishes • Moderately successful attempts at text features	• Serviceable handwriting • Fonts that impair reading moderately • Consistent margins and spacing; a few blemishes • Successful attempts at text features	• Clear, legible handwriting • Appropriate font styles and sizes • Very consistent margins and spacing; neat piece • Well-written and well-placed text features	• Pleasing, easy-to-read handwriting • Pleasing, easy-to-read font styles and sizes • Excellent use of white space; very neat piece throughout • Seamless, appropriate text features throughout

Cut-Apart Scoring Sheets

Piece: _____ Name: _____

Trait	1	2	3	4	5	6
Ideas The piece's content— its central message and details.						
Organization The internal structure of the piece.						
Voice The tone and tenor of the piece—the personal stamp of the writer.						
Word Choice The specific vocabulary the writer uses to convey meaning.						
Sentence Fluency The way words and phrases flow through the piece.						
Conventions The mechanical correctness of the piece.						
Presentation The physical appearance of the piece.						

Write your comments and suggestions on the back of this sheet.

Piece: _____ Name: _____

Trait	1	2	3	4	5	6
Ideas The piece's content— its central message and details.						
Organization The internal structure of the piece.						
Voice The tone and tenor of the piece—the personal stamp of the writer.						
Word Choice The specific vocabulary the writer uses to convey meaning.						
Sentence Fluency The way words and phrases flow through the piece.						
Conventions The mechanical correctness of the piece.						
Presentation The physical appearance of the piece.						

Write your comments and suggestions on the back of this sheet.

Piece: _____ Name: _____

Trait	1	2	3	4	5
Ideas The piece's content— its central message and details.					
Organization The internal structure of the piece.					
Voice The tone and tenor of the piece—the personal stamp of the writer.					
Word Choice The specific vocabulary the writer uses to convey meaning.					
Sentence Fluency The way words and phrases flow through the piece.					
Conventions The mechanical correctness of the piece.					
Presentation The physical appearance of the piece.					

Write your comments and suggestions on the back of this sheet.

Piece: _____ Name: _____

Trait	1	2	3	4
Ideas The piece's content— its central message and details.				
Organization The internal structure of the piece.				
Voice The tone and tenor of the piece—the personal stamp of the writer.				
Word Choice The specific vocabulary the writer uses to convey meaning.				
Sentence Fluency The way words and phrases flow through the piece.				
Conventions The mechanical correctness of the piece.				
Presentation The physical appearance of the piece.				

Write your comments and suggestions on the back of this sheet.

Scoring Guide: Narrative Writing

Narrative writing re-creates a real or imagined experience. It usually contains four elements: characters, a setting, a chronological sequence of events, and a conflict or problem to be solved. The writer typically builds in high points by putting characters into interesting situations, weaving in plot twists, incorporating vivid details, and creating a central conflict or problem that builds suspense and holds the piece together.

6 EXCEPTIONAL

HIGH

- Starts with a lead that sets up the story and draws the reader in.
- Contains characters that are believable, fresh, and well described. The characters grow and learn.
- Describes a setting that is unique and rich.
- Features events that are logically sequenced and move the story forward. Time and place work in harmony.
- Is a complete story that has never been told or is an original twist on a familiar story. The plot is well developed. There is a key conflict or problem that is compelling and eventually solved.
- Features well-used literary techniques, such as foreshadowing and symbolism.
- Leaves the reader feeling intrigued, delighted, surprised, entertained, and/or informed.
- Ends satisfyingly because the key conflict or problem is solved thoughtfully and credibly.

5 STRONG

4 REFINING

MIDDLE

- Starts with a lead that sets the scene, but is predictable or unoriginal.
- Contains characters that are a bit too familiar. The characters show little change in their thinking or understanding as the story moves along.
- Offers a setting that is not described all that well.
- Features events that are given the same level of importance. Significant ones mingle with trivial ones, and sometimes stray from the main story line.
- Is a nearly complete story that may not contain new or original thinking. The plot moves forward, but then stumbles. Minor conflicts and problems distract from major ones.
- Contains examples of literary techniques such as foreshadowing and symbolism that are not all that effective.
- Leaves the reader engaged at some points, detached at others.
- Ends by providing the reader with a sense of resolution, but he or she may also feel unsatisfied or perplexed.

3 DEVELOPING

2 EMERGING

LOW

- Starts with a lead that is perfunctory: "I'm going to tell you about the time…."
- Contains characters that don't feel real. The unconvincing characters are stereotypes or cardboard cutouts.
- Offers a setting that is not at all described clearly and/or completely.
- Features simple, incomplete events that don't relate to one another and/or don't add up to anything much. There is a mismatch between the time and place.
- Is a story that jumps around illogically. There is no clear conflict or problem to be solved.
- Contains no examples of literary techniques—or, at most, poor, purposeless ones.
- Leaves the reader frustrated and/or disappointed. He or she feels the story was not thought out before it was committed to paper.
- Finishes with no clear ending or, at most, a halfhearted attempt at an ending, leaving the reader wondering why he or she bothered to read the piece.

1 RUDIMENTARY

Scoring Guide: Expository Writing

The primary purpose for expository writing is to inform or explain, using reliable and accurate information. Although usually associated with the research report or traditional essay, expository writing needn't always contain "just the facts." The writer might include personal experiences, details from his or her life, to enliven the piece. Strong expository writing has an authoritative, knowledgeable, and confident voice that adds credibility.

6 HIGH

EXCEPTIONAL

- Delves into what really matters about the topic.
- Offers an insider's perspective.
- Provides unexpected or surprising details that go beyond the obvious.
- Is focused, coherent, and well organized.
- Invites the reader to analyze and synthesize details to draw his or her own conclusions.
- Is bursting with fascinating, original facts that are accurate and, when appropriate, linked to a primary source.
- Contains anecdotes that bring the topic to life.
- Anticipates and answers the reader's questions.
- Stays on point and contains a compelling voice until the end.

5 STRONG

---

4 MIDDLE

REFINING

- Provides an overview of the topic and only a few key facts.
- Offers the perspective of an outsider looking in.
- Lacks fresh thinking or surprises. Relies too heavily on common knowledge. Provides mostly mundane, predictable details about the topic.
- Is relatively focused, coherent, and organized. Generally stays on topic.
- Contains focused descriptions, but also fuzzy ones. The writer doesn't consistently connect the dots.
- Includes facts that are somewhat suspicious and not linked to primary sources.
- Features few, if any, anecdotes to bring the topic to life.
- Does not anticipate the reader's questions.
- Speaks in a spotty voice—commanding one moment, cautious the next.

3 DEVELOPING

---

2 LOW

EMERGING

- Misses the main point completely. The writer's purpose is not clear.
- Offers a complete outsider's perspective.
- Contains details that are completely unrelated to the main topic.
- Is unfocused, incoherent, and poorly organized.
- Makes sweeping statements. Nothing new is shared.
- Lacks fascinating, original facts. Any facts the piece does contain are seemingly inaccurate or unsupported.
- Contains no anecdotes to bring the topic to life.
- Does not anticipate the reader's questions. In fact, the piece contains no evidence that the writer has thought about audience at all.
- Requires energy to read from beginning to end.

1 RUDIMENTARY

Scoring Guide: Persuasive Writing

Persuasive writing contains a strong argument based on solid information that convinces the reader to embrace the writer's point of view. Sometimes, persuasive writing is a call to action, such as a donation solicitation from a charitable organization. Other times, it's an attempt to change attitudes, such as an op-ed piece in your local newspaper. Regardless of the format, the writing needs to be clear, compelling, and well supported. The writer should not waver in his or her position.

6 — EXCEPTIONAL (HIGH)

- Influences the reader's thinking through sound reasoning and a compelling argument.
- Contains opinions are that well supported by facts and personal experiences. Differences among opinion, facts, and personal experiences are clear.
- Takes a position that is defensible and logical.
- Exposes weaknesses of other positions.
- Avoids generalities and exaggerations.
- Includes many moments of sound reasoning and judgment.
- Reveals only the best evidence to make the strongest statement possible.
- Connects to a larger "truth."

5 — STRONG

4 — REFINING (MIDDLE)

- Raises questions for the reader, but may fail to persuade him or her because the thinking is superficial and only hints at something deep.
- Mixes opinions, facts, and personal experiences. The piece relies on emotion more than truth. Data may be present, but not used to full effect.
- Contains an argument that starts out strong, but fades. Offers few new insights into the topic.
- Attempts to expose holes in other opinions, with mixed results.
- Features generalities or exaggerations, but also concrete information and clear examples.
- Includes a few moments of sound reasoning and judgment.
- Contains some evidence that hits the mark and some that veers off course.
- Waffles. Many statements are plausible while others are far-fetched, leaving the reader unconvinced.

3 — DEVELOPING

2 — EMERGING (LOW)

- Does not influence the reader. The writer's thinking and reasoning is vulnerable to attack.
- Abounds with opinions that are not supported by facts or personal experiences.
- Takes a position that is not clear or not credible. The argument is illogical or implausible.
- Ignores the opposing side of the argument.
- Offers only generalities and exaggerations—no hard facts that could sway the reader.
- Includes no moments of sound reasoning and judgment.
- Lacks the evidence necessary for the reader to take a stand.
- Does not question or does not probe. The piece misses the target.

1 — RUDIMENTARY

Student Feedback Forms

Name _____ Date _____

Paper Title _____

| **Ideas** | The piece's content—its central message and details that support that message. |

See how strong your ideas are and what to do to improve them.

1	2	3	4	5	6
Getting Started	On Your Way	Making Strides	Almost There	Well Done	Expert

Suggestion for revision:

Name _____ Date _____

Paper Title _____

| **Organization** | The internal structure of the piece—the thread of logic, the pattern of meaning. |

See how strong your organization is and what to do to improve it.

1	2	3	4	5	6
Getting Started	On Your Way	Making Strides	Almost There	Well Done	Expert

Suggestion for revision:

Name _____ Date _____

Paper Title _____

| **Voice** | The tone and tenor of the piece—the personal stamp of the writer. |

See how strong your voice is and what to do to improve it.

1	2	3	4	5	6
Getting Started	On Your Way	Making Strides	Almost There	Well Done	Expert

Suggestion for revision:

Name _____ Date _____

Paper Title _____

| **Word Choice** | The specific vocabulary the writer uses to convey meaning and enlighten the reader. |

See how strong your word choice is and what to do to improve it.

1	2	3	4	5	6
Getting Started	On Your Way	Making Strides	Almost There	Well Done	Expert

Suggestion for revision:

Student Feedback Forms

Name _____ Date _____

Paper Title _____

| Sentence Fluency | The way words and phrases flow through the piece. |

See how strong your sentence fluency is and what to do to improve it.

1	2	3	4	5	6
Getting Started	On Your Way	Making Strides	Almost There	Well Done	Expert

Suggestion for revision:

Name _____ Date _____

Paper Title _____

| Conventions | The mechanical correctness of the piece. Correct use of conventions guides the reader through the text easily. |

See how strong your conventions are and what to do to improve them.

1	2	3	4	5	6
Getting Started	On Your Way	Making Strides	Almost There	Well Done	Expert

Suggestion for editing:

Name _____ Date _____

Paper Title _____

Presentation The physical appearance of the piece. A visually appealing text provides a welcome mat. It invites the reader in.

See how strong your presentation is and what to do to improve it.

1	2	3	4	5	6
Getting Started	On Your Way	Making Strides	Almost There	Well Done	Expert

Suggestion for editing:

Name _____ Date _____

Paper Title _____

How close is this piece to being finished and ready for the reader?

1	2	3	4	5
Not Ready		Almost Ready		Ready

Suggestions for final revision and/or editing:

Ready-to-Publish Checklist

Ideas

☐ Have you chosen a topic that interests you or come up with an interesting way to deal with an assigned topic?

☐ Did you focus the topic so it is manageable?

☐ Have you developed the topic purposefully and with fresh and original thinking?

☐ Have you used accurate and quality details to go beyond the obvious?

Organization

☐ Did you use an effective lead to get the reader's attention?

☐ Did you use a variety of sequence and transition words thoughtfully to connect sentences and paragraphs?

☐ Does the body of your piece develop logically?

☐ Have you wrapped up the writing in the right place and given the reader something more to think about?

Voice

☐ Have you established a tone that suits the writing well?

☐ Is the purpose of your writing clear?

☐ Have you thought about your audience and how best to reach them?

☐ What have you done to make your writing fresh and original?

Word Choice

☐ Have you used strong verbs throughout your piece?

☐ Do some of your words and phrases stand out?

☐ Are these the very best words you can think of to express your ideas clearly?

☐ Have you chosen words thoughtfully, without unnecessary repetition?

Sentence Fluency

☐ Did you start your sentences differently and vary their lengths?

☐ Have you used a variety of sentence types?

☐ Do your sentences flow smoothly and are they easy to read aloud?

☐ What did you do to stretch how you used sentences in this piece?

Conventions

☐ Are your words spelled correctly?

☐ Did you punctuate effectively and paragraph accurately?

☐ Did you apply the rules of capitalization throughout your piece?

☐ Does your grammar and usage reflect the use of standard English?

Presentation

☐ Is your handwriting neat and legible?

☐ Did you pick a readable font and font size?

☐ Have you made good use of white space on the page so your piece is easy to read?

☐ Did you add text features to help the reader better understand or navigate the piece?

Record-Keeping and Planning Forms

One challenge teachers face is keeping track of what students are writing and how it is progressing. Students will likely be at different places in the writing process at any given time—prewriting, drafting, conferring, revising, editing, and publishing. The teacher-friendly forms in this section will help. The record-keeping forms on pages 34 and 35 enable you to document growth ascertained using the Student Writing Record form on pages 36–39 and the Teacher Contact Record form on page 40. Use the planning forms to organize weekly lessons and prepare for conferences with individual students or small groups.

Record-Keeping Form for Individual Students

This full-page form is used for tracking the scores individual students earn on writing assignments over time. For each piece, circle the appropriate scores and determine an average score to record in your grade book, if you wish. The form enables you to see at a glance the traits in which the student is improving and/or those in which he or she might need more instruction and support.

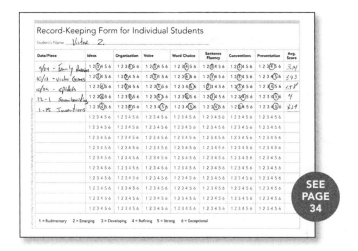

Record-Keeping Form for the Whole Class

This full-page form is used for tracking the scores the class earns on a specific writing assignment. For each student, circle the appropriate scores and determine an average score to record in your grade book, if you wish. This form enables you to see at a glance the traits in which students show strengths and weaknesses on one piece so that you can plan follow-up instruction more effectively.

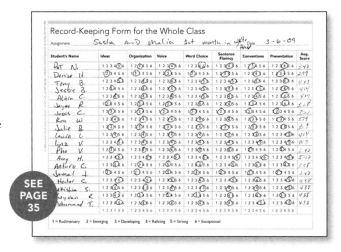

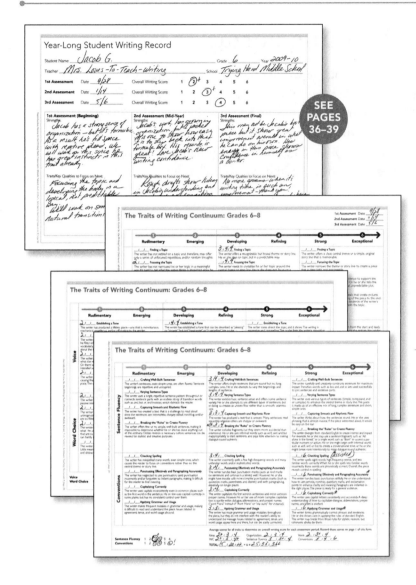

SEE PAGES 36–39

Year-Long Student Writing Record

Use this four-page form to track student writing progress from the beginning of the year to the end. Collect and assess three samples of writing, at the beginning, middle, and end of the year, and write goals for the student after each assessment. For each assessment period, use a different color pen for filling in the date, scores, and comments to pinpoint key information and track progress at a glance—for instance, green for the beginning of the year, red for the middle, and blue for the end.

The filled-out form, along with the samples of work and the assessment, can be placed in a folder and shared with parents. At the end of the year, pass the folder to the student's new teacher. That way, at the first conference of the following year, the student's new teacher can review the previous year's folder with parents, and share the beginning-of-the-year assessment results, as noted on a new Year-Long Student Writing Record form.

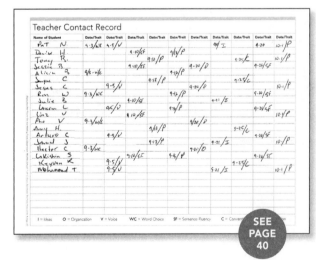

SEE PAGE 40

Teacher Contact Record

As the year progresses, you'll want to make sure that you have made time to talk to students in your class about how their writing is developing in all the traits. This handy, one-page form can be used to document the writing contacts you have with students, individually and in small groups. Use it to capture the interactions you have with each student during the course of the year. You'll see at a glance where students are having the most trouble, and where you have spent time helping them.

Weekly Lesson Plan Form

This form helps you think about traits of writing and modes of writing (narrative, expository, and persuasive) simultaneously as you plan your weekly lessons. There's plenty of space to fill in details for each day of the week. Just photocopy completed forms and clip them together to create a collection of trait-based, mode-specific writing lessons. You can also scan them into a computer file and store them electronically for later use.

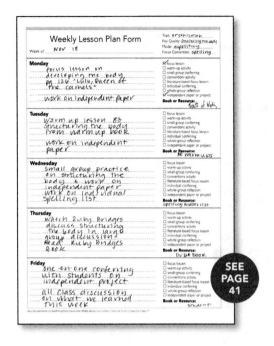

Modes of Writing Conference Planners

Once you've scored a student's narrative, expository, or persuasive paper, give the appropriate two-page conference planner to him or her, with the trait or traits highlighted that you'd like him or her to address. The planner will help the writer prepare for a conference by thinking through changes or revisions that might be made to the next draft.

Record-Keeping Form for Individual Students

Student's Name _____

Date/Piece	Ideas	Organization	Voice	Word Choice	Sentence Fluency	Conventions	Presentation	Avg. Score
	1 2 3 4 5 6	1 2 3 4 5 6	1 2 3 4 5 6	1 2 3 4 5 6	1 2 3 4 5 6	1 2 3 4 5 6	1 2 3 4 5 6	
	1 2 3 4 5 6	1 2 3 4 5 6	1 2 3 4 5 6	1 2 3 4 5 6	1 2 3 4 5 6	1 2 3 4 5 6	1 2 3 4 5 6	
	1 2 3 4 5 6	1 2 3 4 5 6	1 2 3 4 5 6	1 2 3 4 5 6	1 2 3 4 5 6	1 2 3 4 5 6	1 2 3 4 5 6	
	1 2 3 4 5 6	1 2 3 4 5 6	1 2 3 4 5 6	1 2 3 4 5 6	1 2 3 4 5 6	1 2 3 4 5 6	1 2 3 4 5 6	
	1 2 3 4 5 6	1 2 3 4 5 6	1 2 3 4 5 6	1 2 3 4 5 6	1 2 3 4 5 6	1 2 3 4 5 6	1 2 3 4 5 6	
	1 2 3 4 5 6	1 2 3 4 5 6	1 2 3 4 5 6	1 2 3 4 5 6	1 2 3 4 5 6	1 2 3 4 5 6	1 2 3 4 5 6	
	1 2 3 4 5 6	1 2 3 4 5 6	1 2 3 4 5 6	1 2 3 4 5 6	1 2 3 4 5 6	1 2 3 4 5 6	1 2 3 4 5 6	
	1 2 3 4 5 6	1 2 3 4 5 6	1 2 3 4 5 6	1 2 3 4 5 6	1 2 3 4 5 6	1 2 3 4 5 6	1 2 3 4 5 6	
	1 2 3 4 5 6	1 2 3 4 5 6	1 2 3 4 5 6	1 2 3 4 5 6	1 2 3 4 5 6	1 2 3 4 5 6	1 2 3 4 5 6	
	1 2 3 4 5 6	1 2 3 4 5 6	1 2 3 4 5 6	1 2 3 4 5 6	1 2 3 4 5 6	1 2 3 4 5 6	1 2 3 4 5 6	
	1 2 3 4 5 6	1 2 3 4 5 6	1 2 3 4 5 6	1 2 3 4 5 6	1 2 3 4 5 6	1 2 3 4 5 6	1 2 3 4 5 6	
	1 2 3 4 5 6	1 2 3 4 5 6	1 2 3 4 5 6	1 2 3 4 5 6	1 2 3 4 5 6	1 2 3 4 5 6	1 2 3 4 5 6	
	1 2 3 4 5 6	1 2 3 4 5 6	1 2 3 4 5 6	1 2 3 4 5 6	1 2 3 4 5 6	1 2 3 4 5 6	1 2 3 4 5 6	
	1 2 3 4 5 6	1 2 3 4 5 6	1 2 3 4 5 6	1 2 3 4 5 6	1 2 3 4 5 6	1 2 3 4 5 6	1 2 3 4 5 6	
	1 2 3 4 5 6	1 2 3 4 5 6	1 2 3 4 5 6	1 2 3 4 5 6	1 2 3 4 5 6	1 2 3 4 5 6	1 2 3 4 5 6	
	1 2 3 4 5 6	1 2 3 4 5 6	1 2 3 4 5 6	1 2 3 4 5 6	1 2 3 4 5 6	1 2 3 4 5 6	1 2 3 4 5 6	
	1 2 3 4 5 6	1 2 3 4 5 6	1 2 3 4 5 6	1 2 3 4 5 6	1 2 3 4 5 6	1 2 3 4 5 6	1 2 3 4 5 6	
	1 2 3 4 5 6	1 2 3 4 5 6	1 2 3 4 5 6	1 2 3 4 5 6	1 2 3 4 5 6	1 2 3 4 5 6	1 2 3 4 5 6	

1 = Rudimentary   2 = Emerging   3 = Developing   4 = Refining   5 = Strong   6 = Exceptional

Record-Keeping Form for the Whole Class

Assignment _____   Date _____

Student's Name	Ideas	Organization	Voice	Word Choice	Sentence Fluency	Conventions	Presentation	Avg. Score
	1 2 3 4 5 6	1 2 3 4 5 6	1 2 3 4 5 6	1 2 3 4 5 6	1 2 3 4 5 6	1 2 3 4 5 6	1 2 3 4 5 6	
	1 2 3 4 5 6	1 2 3 4 5 6	1 2 3 4 5 6	1 2 3 4 5 6	1 2 3 4 5 6	1 2 3 4 5 6	1 2 3 4 5 6	
	1 2 3 4 5 6	1 2 3 4 5 6	1 2 3 4 5 6	1 2 3 4 5 6	1 2 3 4 5 6	1 2 3 4 5 6	1 2 3 4 5 6	
	1 2 3 4 5 6	1 2 3 4 5 6	1 2 3 4 5 6	1 2 3 4 5 6	1 2 3 4 5 6	1 2 3 4 5 6	1 2 3 4 5 6	
	1 2 3 4 5 6	1 2 3 4 5 6	1 2 3 4 5 6	1 2 3 4 5 6	1 2 3 4 5 6	1 2 3 4 5 6	1 2 3 4 5 6	
	1 2 3 4 5 6	1 2 3 4 5 6	1 2 3 4 5 6	1 2 3 4 5 6	1 2 3 4 5 6	1 2 3 4 5 6	1 2 3 4 5 6	
	1 2 3 4 5 6	1 2 3 4 5 6	1 2 3 4 5 6	1 2 3 4 5 6	1 2 3 4 5 6	1 2 3 4 5 6	1 2 3 4 5 6	
	1 2 3 4 5 6	1 2 3 4 5 6	1 2 3 4 5 6	1 2 3 4 5 6	1 2 3 4 5 6	1 2 3 4 5 6	1 2 3 4 5 6	
	1 2 3 4 5 6	1 2 3 4 5 6	1 2 3 4 5 6	1 2 3 4 5 6	1 2 3 4 5 6	1 2 3 4 5 6	1 2 3 4 5 6	
	1 2 3 4 5 6	1 2 3 4 5 6	1 2 3 4 5 6	1 2 3 4 5 6	1 2 3 4 5 6	1 2 3 4 5 6	1 2 3 4 5 6	
	1 2 3 4 5 6	1 2 3 4 5 6	1 2 3 4 5 6	1 2 3 4 5 6	1 2 3 4 5 6	1 2 3 4 5 6	1 2 3 4 5 6	
	1 2 3 4 5 6	1 2 3 4 5 6	1 2 3 4 5 6	1 2 3 4 5 6	1 2 3 4 5 6	1 2 3 4 5 6	1 2 3 4 5 6	
	1 2 3 4 5 6	1 2 3 4 5 6	1 2 3 4 5 6	1 2 3 4 5 6	1 2 3 4 5 6	1 2 3 4 5 6	1 2 3 4 5 6	
	1 2 3 4 5 6	1 2 3 4 5 6	1 2 3 4 5 6	1 2 3 4 5 6	1 2 3 4 5 6	1 2 3 4 5 6	1 2 3 4 5 6	
	1 2 3 4 5 6	1 2 3 4 5 6	1 2 3 4 5 6	1 2 3 4 5 6	1 2 3 4 5 6	1 2 3 4 5 6	1 2 3 4 5 6	
	1 2 3 4 5 6	1 2 3 4 5 6	1 2 3 4 5 6	1 2 3 4 5 6	1 2 3 4 5 6	1 2 3 4 5 6	1 2 3 4 5 6	
	1 2 3 4 5 6	1 2 3 4 5 6	1 2 3 4 5 6	1 2 3 4 5 6	1 2 3 4 5 6	1 2 3 4 5 6	1 2 3 4 5 6	
	1 2 3 4 5 6	1 2 3 4 5 6	1 2 3 4 5 6	1 2 3 4 5 6	1 2 3 4 5 6	1 2 3 4 5 6	1 2 3 4 5 6	
	1 2 3 4 5 6	1 2 3 4 5 6	1 2 3 4 5 6	1 2 3 4 5 6	1 2 3 4 5 6	1 2 3 4 5 6	1 2 3 4 5 6	
	1 2 3 4 5 6	1 2 3 4 5 6	1 2 3 4 5 6	1 2 3 4 5 6	1 2 3 4 5 6	1 2 3 4 5 6	1 2 3 4 5 6	
	1 2 3 4 5 6	1 2 3 4 5 6	1 2 3 4 5 6	1 2 3 4 5 6	1 2 3 4 5 6	1 2 3 4 5 6	1 2 3 4 5 6	
	1 2 3 4 5 6	1 2 3 4 5 6	1 2 3 4 5 6	1 2 3 4 5 6	1 2 3 4 5 6	1 2 3 4 5 6	1 2 3 4 5 6	

1 = Rudimentary   2 = Emerging   3 = Developing   4 = Refining   5 = Strong   6 = Exceptional

Year-Long Student Writing Record

Student Name _____ Grade _____ Year _____

Teacher _____ School _____

1st Assessment	Date _____	Overall Writing Score:	1	2	3	4	5	6
2nd Assessment	Date _____	Overall Writing Score:	1	2	3	4	5	6
3rd Assessment	Date _____	Overall Writing Score:	1	2	3	4	5	6

1st Assessment (Beginning)
Strengths:

Traits/Key Qualities to Focus on Next:

2nd Assessment (Mid-Year)
Strengths:

Traits/Key Qualities to Focus on Next:

3rd Assessment (Final)
Strengths:

Traits/Key Qualities to Focus on Next:

The Traits of Writing Continuum: Grades 6-8

	1 Rudimentary / 2 Emerging	3 Developing / 4 Refining	5 Strong / 6 Exceptional

Ideas

1 Rudimentary — 2 Emerging

Finding a Topic
___/___/___ The writer has not settled on a topic and, therefore, may offer only a series of unfocused, repetitious, and/or random thoughts.

Focusing the Topic
___/___/___ The writer has not narrowed his or her topic in a meaningful way. It's hard to tell what the writer thinks is important since he or she devotes equal importance to each piece of information.

Developing the Topic
___/___/___ The writer has created a piece that is so short the reader cannot fully understand or appreciate what he or she wants to say. He or she may have simply restated an assigned topic or responded to a prompt without devoting much thought or effort to it.

Using Details
___/___/___ The writer has clearly devoted little attention to details. The writing contains limited or completely inaccurate information. After reading the piece, the reader is left with many unanswered questions.

3 Developing — 4 Refining

Finding a Topic
___/___/___ The writer offers a recognizable but broad theme or story line. He or she stays on topic, but in a predictable way.

Focusing the Topic
___/___/___ The writer needs to crystallize his or her topic around the central theme or story line. He or she does not focus on a specific aspect of the topic.

Developing the Topic
___/___/___ The writer draws on personal knowledge and experience, but does not offer a unique perspective. He or she does not probe deeply, but instead gives the reader only a glimpse at aspects of the topic.

Using Details
___/___/___ The writer offers details, but they do not always hit the mark because they are inaccurate or irrelevant. He or she does not create a picture in the reader's mind because key questions about the central theme or story line have not been addressed.

5 Strong — 6 Exceptional

Finding a Topic
___/___/___ The writer offers a clear, central theme or a simple, original story line that is memorable.

Focusing the Topic
___/___/___ The writer narrows the theme or story line to create a piece that is clear, tight, and manageable.

Developing the Topic
___/___/___ The writer provides enough critical evidence to support the theme and shows insight on the topic. Or he or she tells the story in a fresh way through an original, unpredictable plot.

Using Details
___/___/___ The writer offers credible, accurate details that create pictures in the reader's mind, from the beginning of the piece to the end. Those details provide the reader with evidence of the writer's knowledge about and/or experience with the topic.

Organization

1 Rudimentary — 2 Emerging

Creating the Lead
___/___/___ The writer does not give the reader any clue about what is to come. The opening point feels as if it were chosen randomly.

Using Sequence Words and Transition Words
___/___/___ The writer does not provide sequence and/or transition words between sections or provides words that are so confusing the reader is unable to sort one section from another.

Structuring the Body
___/___/___ The writer does not show clearly what comes first, next, and last, making it difficult to understand how sections fit together. The writer slows down when he or she should speed up, and speeds up when he or she should slow down.

Ending With a Sense of Resolution
___/___/___ The writer ends the piece with no conclusion at all—or nothing more than "The End" or something equally bland. There is no sense of resolution, no sense of completion.

3 Developing — 4 Refining

Creating the Lead
___/___/___ The writer presents an introduction, although it may not be original or thought-provoking. Instead, it may be a simple restatement of the topic and, therefore, does not create a sense of anticipation about what is to come.

Using Sequence Words and Transition Words
___/___/___ The writer uses sequence words to show the logical order of details, but they feel obvious or canned. The use of transition words is spotty and rarely creates coherence.

Structuring the Body
___/___/___ The writer sequences events and important points logically, for the most part. However, the reader may wish to move a few things around to create a more sensible flow. He or she may also feel the urge to speed up or slow down for more satisfying pacing.

Ending With a Sense of Resolution
___/___/___ The writer ends the piece on a familiar note: "Thank you for reading . . ." "Now you know all about . . ." or "They lived happily ever after." He or she needs to tie up loose ends to leave the reader with a sense of satisfaction or closure.

5 Strong — 6 Exceptional

Creating the Lead
___/___/___ The writer grabs the reader's attention from the start and leads him or her into the piece naturally. He or she entices the reader, providing a tantalizing glimpse of what is to come.

Using Sequence Words and Transition Words
___/___/___ The writer includes a variety of carefully selected sequence words (such as *later, then,* and *meanwhile*) and transition words (such as *however, also,* and *clearly*), which are placed wisely to guide the reader through the piece by showing how ideas progress, relate, and/or diverge.

Structuring the Body
___/___/___ The writer creates a piece that is easy to follow by fitting details together logically. He or she slows down to spotlight important points or events, and speeds up when he or she needs to move the reader along.

Ending With a Sense of Resolution
___/___/___ The writer sums up his or her thinking in a natural, thoughtful, and convincing way. He or she anticipates and answers any lingering questions the reader may have, providing a strong sense of closure.

	1	2	3	4	5	6
Ideas	1	2	3	4	5	6
Organization	1	2	3	4	5	6

The Traits of Writing Continuum: Grades 6–8

	Rudimentary (1) — Emerging (2)	Developing (3) — Refining (4)	Strong (5) — Exceptional (6)
Voice	**Establishing a Tone** / / / The writer has produced a lifeless piece—one that is monotonous, mechanical, repetitious, and/or off-putting to the reader.	**Establishing a Tone** / / / The writer has established a tone that can be described as "pleasing" or "sincere," but not "passionate" or "compelling." He or she attempts to create a tone that hits the mark, but the overall result feels generic.	**Establishing a Tone** / / / The writer cares about the topic, and it shows. The writing is expressive and compelling. The reader feels the writer's conviction, authority, and integrity.
	Conveying the Purpose / / / The writer chose the topic for mysterious reasons. The piece may be filled with random thoughts, technical jargon, or inappropriate vocabulary, making it impossible to discern how the writer feels about the topic.	**Conveying the Purpose** / / / The writer has chosen a voice for the piece that is not completely clear. There are only a few moments when the reader understands where the writer is coming from and why he or she wrote the piece.	**Conveying the Purpose** / / / The writer makes clear his or her reason for creating the piece. He or she offers a point of view that is appropriate for the mode (narrative, expository, or persuasive), which compels the reader to read on.
	Creating a Connection to the Audience / / / The writer provides no evidence that he or she has considered what the reader might need to know to connect with the topic. Or there is an obvious mismatch between the piece's tone and the intended audience.	**Creating a Connection to the Audience** / / / The writer keeps the reader at a distance. The connection between reader and writer is tenuous because the writer reveals little about what is important or meaningful about the topic.	**Creating a Connection to the Audience** / / / The writer speaks in a way that makes the reader want to listen. He or she has considered what the reader needs to know and the best way to convey it by sharing his or her fascination, feelings, and opinions about the topic.
	Taking Risks to Create Voice / / / The writer creates no highs and lows. The piece is flat and lifeless, causing the reader to wonder why he or she wrote it in the first place. The writer's voice does not pop out, even for a moment.	**Taking Risks to Create Voice** / / / The writer creates a few moments that catch the reader's attention, but only a few. The piece sounds like anyone could have written it. It lacks the energy, commitment, and conviction that would distinguish it from other pieces on the same topic.	**Taking Risks to Create Voice** / / / The writer expresses ideas in new ways, which makes the piece interesting and original. The writing sounds like the writer because of his or her use of distinctive, just-right words and phrases.
Word Choice	**Applying Strong Verbs** / / / The writer makes no attempt at selecting verbs with energy. The passive voice dominates the piece.	**Applying Strong Verbs** / / / The writer uses the passive voice quite a bit and includes few "action words" to give the piece energy.	**Applying Strong Verbs** / / / The writer uses many "action words," giving the piece punch and pizzazz. He or she has stretched to find lively verbs that add energy to the piece.
	Selecting Striking Words and Phrases / / / The writer uses words that are repetitive, vague, and/or unimaginative. Limited meaning comes through because the words are so lifeless.	**Selecting Striking Words and Phrases** / / / The writer provides little evidence that he or she has stretched for the best words or phrases. He or she may have attempted to use literary techniques, but they are clichés for the most part.	**Selecting Striking Words and Phrases** / / / The writer uses many finely honed words and phrases. His or her creative and effective use of literary techniques such as alliteration, simile, and metaphor makes the piece a pleasure to read.
	Using Specific and Accurate Words / / / The writer misuses words, making it difficult to understand what what he or she is attempting to convey. Or he or she uses words that are so technical, inappropriate, or irrelevant the average reader can hardly understand what he or she is saying.	**Using Specific and Accurate Words** / / / The writer presents specific and accurate words, except for those related to sophisticated and/or content-related topics. Technical or irrelevant jargon is off-putting to the reader. The words rarely capture the reader's imagination.	**Using Specific and Accurate Words** / / / The writer uses words with precision. He or she selects words the reader needs to fully understand the message. The writer chooses nouns, adjectives, adverbs, and so forth that create clarity and bring the topic to life.
	Choosing Words That Deepen Meaning / / / The writer uses many words and phrases that simply do not work. Little meaning comes through because the language is so imprecise and distracting.	**Choosing Words That Deepen Meaning** / / / The writer fills the piece with unoriginal language rather than language that results from careful revision. The words communicate the basic idea, but they are ordinary and uninspired.	**Choosing Words That Deepen Meaning** / / / The writer uses words to capture the reader's imagination and enhance the piece's meaning. There is a deliberate attempt to choose the best word over the first word that comes to mind.

Voice   1 2 3 4 5 6
Word Choice 1 2 3 4 5 6

The Traits of Writing Continuum: Grades 6–8

1 Rudimentary	2 Emerging	3 Developing	4 Refining	5 Strong	6 Exceptional

Sentence Fluency

Crafting Well-Built Sentences

___/___/___ (1–2) The writer's sentences, even simple ones, are often flawed. Sentence beginnings are repetitive and uninspired.

___/___/___ (3–4) The writer offers simple sentences that are sound but no long, complex ones. He or she attempts to vary the beginnings and lengths of sentences.

___/___/___ (5–6) The writer carefully and creatively constructs sentences for maximum impact. Transition words such as *but, and,* and *so* are used successfully to join sentences and sentence parts.

Varying Sentence Types

___/___/___ (1–2) The writer uses a single, repetitive sentence pattern throughout or connects sentence parts with an endless string of transition words such as *and, but, or,* and *because,* which distracts the reader.

___/___/___ (3–4) The writer exhibits basic sentence sense and offers some sentence variety. He or she attempts to use different types of sentences, but in doing so creates an uneven flow rather than a smooth, seamless one.

___/___/___ (5–6) The writer uses various types of sentences (simple, compound, and/or complex) to enhance the central theme or story line. The piece is made up of an effective mix of long, complex sentences and short, simple ones.

Capturing Smooth and Rhythmic Flow

___/___/___ (1–2) The writer has created a text that is a challenge to read aloud since the sentences are incomplete, choppy, stilted, rambling, and/or awkward.

___/___/___ (3–4) The writer has produced a text that is uneven. Many sentences read smoothly, whereas others are choppy or awkward.

___/___/___ (5–6) The writer thinks about how the sentences sound. He or she uses phrasing that is almost musical. If the piece were read aloud, it would be easy on the ear.

Breaking the "Rules" to Create Fluency

___/___/___ (1–2) The writer offers few or no simple, well-built sentences, making it impossible to determine whether he or she has done anything out of the ordinary. Global revision is necessary before sentences can be revised for stylistic and creative purposes.

___/___/___ (3–4) The writer includes fragments, but they seem more accidental than intentional. He or she uses informal words such as *well, and,* and *but* inappropriately to start sentences, and pays little attention to making dialogue sound authentic.

___/___/___ (5–6) The writer diverges from standard English to create interest and impact. For example, he or she may use a sentence fragment, such as "All alone in the forest," or a single word, such as "Bam!" to accent a particular moment or action. He or she might begin with informal words such as *well, and,* or *but* to create a conversational tone, or he or she might break rules intentionally to make dialogue sound authentic.

Conventions

Checking Spelling

___/___/___ (1–2) The writer has misspelled many words, even simple ones, which causes the reader to focus on conventions rather than on the central theme or story line.

___/___/___ (3–4) The writer incorrectly spells a few high-frequency words and many unfamiliar words and/or sophisticated words.

___/___/___ (5–6) The writer spells sight words, high-frequency words, and less familiar words correctly. When he or she spells less familiar words incorrectly, those words are phonetically correct. Overall, the piece reveals control in spelling.

Punctuating Effectively and Paragraphing Accurately

___/___/___ (1–2) The writer has neglected to use punctuation, used punctuation incorrectly, and/or forgotten to indent paragraphs, making it difficult for the reader to find meaning.

___/___/___ (3–4) The writer handles basic punctuation marks (such as end marks on sentences and commas in a series) well. However, he or she might have trouble with more complex punctuation marks (such as quotation marks, parentheses, and dashes) and with paragraphing, especially on longer pieces.

___/___/___ (5–6) The writer handles basic punctuation skillfully. He or she understands how to use periods, commas, questions marks, and exclamation points to enhance clarity and meaning. Paragraphs are indented in the right places. The piece is ready for a general audience.

Capitalizing Correctly

___/___/___ (1–2) The writer uses capitals inconsistently even in common places such as the first word in the sentence. He or she uses capitals correctly in some places but has no consistent control over them.

___/___/___ (3–4) The writer capitalizes the first word in sentences and most common proper names. However, his or her use of more complex capitalization is spotty within dialogue, abbreviations, and proper names ("aunt Maria" instead of "Aunt Maria" or "my aunt," for instance).

___/___/___ (5–6) The writer uses capital letters consistently and accurately. A deep understanding of how to capitalize dialogue, abbreviations, proper names, and titles is evident.

Applying Grammar and Usage

___/___/___ (1–2) The writer makes frequent mistakes in grammar and usage, making it difficult to read and understand the piece. Issues related to agreement, tense, and word usage abound.

___/___/___ (3–4) The writer has made grammar and usage mistakes throughout the piece, but they do not interfere with the reader's ability to understand the message. Issues related to agreement, tense, and word usage appear here and there, but can be easily corrected.

___/___/___ (5–6) The writer forms grammatically correct phrases and sentences. He or she shows care in applying the rules of standard English. The writer may break from those rules for stylistic reasons, but otherwise abides by them.

Average scores for all traits to determine an overall writing score for each assessment period. Record those scores on page 1 of this form.

Ideas ___/___/___ Organization ___/___/___ Voice ___/___/___

WC ___/___/___ Sentence Fluency ___/___/___ Conventions ___/___/___

TOTAL: ___/___/___ ÷ 6 = ___/___/___

Sentence Fluency   1   2   3   4   5   6

Conventions   1   2   3   4   5   6

Teacher Contact Record

Name of Student	Date/Trait	Date/Trait	Date/Trait	Date/Trait	Date/Trait	Date/Trait	Date/Trait	Date/Trait	Date/Trait	Date/Trait

I = Ideas   **O** = Organization   **V** = Voice   **WC** = Word Choice   **SF** = Sentence Fluency   **C** = Conventions   **P** = Presentation

Weekly Lesson Plan Form

Trait: _____

Key Quality: _____

Mode: _____

Focus Convention: _____

Week of _____

Monday

- -
- -
- -
- -
- -

☐ focus lesson
☐ warm-up activity
☐ small-group conferring
☐ conventions activity
☐ literature-based focus lesson
☐ individual conferring
☐ whole-group reflection
☐ independent paper or project

Book or Resource:

Tuesday

- -
- -
- -
- -
- -

☐ focus lesson
☐ warm-up activity
☐ small-group conferring
☐ conventions activity
☐ literature-based focus lesson
☐ individual conferring
☐ whole-group reflection
☐ independent paper or project

Book or Resource:

Wednesday

- -
- -
- -
- -
- -

☐ focus lesson
☐ warm-up activity
☐ small-group conferring
☐ conventions activity
☐ literature-based focus lesson
☐ individual conferring
☐ whole-group reflection
☐ independent paper or project

Book or Resource:

Thursday

- -
- -
- -
- -
- -

☐ focus lesson
☐ warm-up activity
☐ small-group conferring
☐ conventions activity
☐ literature-based focus lesson
☐ individual conferring
☐ whole-group reflection
☐ independent paper or project

Book or Resource:

Friday

- -
- -
- -
- -

☐ focus lesson
☐ warm-up activity
☐ small-group conferring
☐ conventions activity
☐ literature-based focus lesson
☐ individual conferring
☐ whole-group reflection
☐ independent paper or project

Book or Resource:

Narrative Writing Conference Planner

Name _____   Class _____

Before our conference on your narrative piece, read the list of questions and directions after the trait(s) that I've highlighted on this sheet. We'll review your responses in the conference.

Ideas

Finding a Topic: What is the controlling idea for your narrative?	**Focusing the Topic:** What problem did you set out to resolve?
Developing the Topic: List at least three elements from the body of your piece that make it a complete narrative.	**Using Details:** Underline several sensory details (sight, touch, taste, smell, hearing) you feel work well in your narrative.

Organization

Creating the Lead: Circle the type of lead you used in your narrative.

analogy or comparison	anecdote or case history	direct address	fact
metaphor	description	one word/phrase	controversial statement
statistic	summary	other:	

Using Sequence Words and Transition Words: Using a highlighter, mark the sequence words and phrases. Then, using a highlighter of a different color, mark the transition words and phrases.

Structuring the Body: Circle a place in your narrative that shows you were thinking about pacing as you wrote.

Ending With a Sense of Resolution: Circle the type of ending you used in your narrative.

epiphany	moral	image	irony
tragedy	surprise	Hollywood ending	other:

Voice

Establishing a Tone: Circle a place where you've established a specific tone and name it here.

Conveying the Purpose: List specific narrative elements (characters, setting, plot) you included in your paper that contribute to its voice.

Creating a Connection to the Audience

Who is your audience?	Name the voice you used to address that audience specifically:

Taking Risks to Create Voice: Put a star next to a place in your narrative where you stretched and took a risk to create voice.

Word Choice

Applying Strong Verbs: Circle "to be" and other verbs that could be made stronger. Write the new verbs above the original ones.

Selecting Striking Words and Phrases: Have you used any figurative language in your narrative? Put a box around examples.

Using Specific and Accurate Words: Highlight any words that you feel are perfect for describing the people, places, and things in your narrative.

Choosing Words That Deepen Meaning: Underline two examples of words or phrases you changed or added to make a part of your narrative clearer and/or more meaningful.

Sentence Fluency

Crafting Well-Built Sentences: Circle the sentence beginnings in your narrative. How alike are they? Underline the ones that should be revised.

Varying Sentence Types: Put a 1 by any simple sentences, a 2 by any compound sentences, a 3 by any complex sentences, and a 4 by any compound-complex sentences in your narrative. Do you have enough variety? If not, revise.

Capturing Smooth and Rhythmic Flow: Read your piece aloud to a classmate. Put a check mark next to any place the writing does not flow as well as you'd like.

Breaking the "Rules" to Create Fluency: What "out of the box" techniques did you try to improve your narrative's sentence fluency?

Conventions

Checking Spelling: List three or more words you stretched to spell correctly.

Punctuating Effectively and Paragraphing Accurately: Put a box around any punctuation you used for stylistic reasons.

Capitalizing Correctly: Double-check to make sure you capitalized all proper nouns and words at the beginning of your sentences. Circle the words in your title that are capitalized correctly.

Applying Grammar and Usage:

Do your subjects and verbs agree? Give an example.	
Do your pronouns and antecedents match? Give an example.	

Presentation

Applying Handwriting Skills: Highlight the section that is easiest to read. Underline the section that would most benefit from better handwriting.

Using Word Processing Effectively: What font and size did you choose?

Is the font easy to read?	Is it appropriate for your audience?

Making Good Use of White Space: Make sure your margins neatly frame the text. Did you leave room around the edges? Did you double-space the text, if requested?

Refining Text Features: List text features you used, such as title, subheadings, page numbers, page headers or footers, and bulleted lists.

Overall

Circle the trait you used most effectively in your narrative piece.			
Ideas	Organization	Voice	Word Choice
Sentence Fluency	Conventions	Presentation	
Explain why:			

Circle the trait you used least effectively in your narrative piece.			
Ideas	Organization	Voice	Word Choice
Sentence Fluency	Conventions	Presentation	
Explain why:			

What is your plan for improving upon the trait you feel needs the most work?

Expository Writing Conference Planner

Name _____ Class _____

Before our conference on your expository piece, read the list of questions and directions after the trait(s) that I've highlighted on this sheet. We'll review your responses in the conference.

Ideas

Finding a Topic: What is your expository paper's topic? Underline it in the first paragraph. If you can't find it, revise the paragraph.	**Focusing the Topic:** Underline the key points you make about this topic. You should have more than one.
Developing the Topic: Will your expository piece leave your reader with questions about the topic? List one or two things she or he might still need to know.	**Using Details:** Have you included credible details in your piece, gleaned from reliable sources? List the sources for those details here.

Organization

Creating the Lead: Circle the type of lead you used in your expository piece.

analogy or comparison	anecdote or case history	direct address	fact
metaphor	description	one word/phrase	controversial statement
statistic	summary	other:	

Using Sequence Words and Transition Words: Circle common sequence and transition words such as *first, second, next, finally, plus,* and *another*. Revise some of them to be more thoughtful and less superficial.

Structuring the Body: Put a star next to the point in your piece where you slowed down to give more information.

Ending With a Sense of Resolution: Did you tie all your details together with an effective type of ending? Circle the type of ending you used.

summary	call-back	thematic reprise	encouraging message
quotation	Ta-da!	other:	

Voice

Establishing a Tone: Name the tone you set out to establish in this piece:

Circle where it comes through the strongest.

Conveying the Purpose: Star at least three places in your piece that convey its purpose by providing specific information.

Creating a Connection to the Audience: Who is your audience?

What did you do in particular to address this audience?

Taking Risks to Create Voice: Did you push to express yourself in a credible yet interesting way? If so, highlight a section that proves it.

Word Choice

Applying Strong Verbs: Name the five strongest verbs you used that show you understand this topic well.

Selecting Striking Words and Phrases: Circle any words and phrases that help to explain this topic particularly well.

Using Specific and Accurate Words: Underline words and phrases that are specific to this topic and might not be used to explain any other topic.

Choosing Words That Deepen Meaning: Highlight a place in the writing where you've used words that help the reader make a deeper connection to the topic.

Sentence Fluency

Crafting Well-Built Sentences: Count the number of words in each sentence. How many sentences are close to the same length? Star two that could be combined to make a longer one.

Varying Sentence Types: Label each of your simple sentences with a 1, compound sentences with a 2, complex sentences with a 3, and compound-complex sentences with a 4. Put a star by the type of sentence you used most often.

Capturing Smooth and Rhythmic Flow: Read your piece aloud to a partner. Put a check by any section that needs to be smoothed out.

Breaking the "Rules" to Create Fluency: Did you construct any sentences in an unexpected way to add interest to your piece? Any fragments? Any exclamations? Any interjections? Any natural-sounding dialogue? If so, circle them.

Conventions

Checking Spelling: What topic-specific words did you use? Circle them and check their spelling.

Punctuating Effectively and Paragraphing Accurately: If you copied what someone else said or wrote, did you set off his or her words in quotation marks? Check to make sure you cited the source. How many paragraphs did you write? Do you have one for an introduction and one for the conclusion? How many others did you include?

Capitalizing Correctly: Check the beginnings of your sentences and the proper nouns for capitals. Highlight any you are not sure about.

Applying Grammar and Usage: Have you followed the rules of standard English? Underline any parts that are examples of informal language you may have included for a particular reason and explain.

Presentation

Applying Handwriting Skills: Highlight the section that is easiest to read. Underline the section that would most benefit from better handwriting.

Using Word Processing Effectively: What font and size did you choose?

Is the font easy to read?	Is it appropriate for your audience?

Making Good Use of White Space: Make sure your margins neatly frame the text. Did you leave room around the edges? Did you double-space the text, if requested?

Refining Text Features: List text features you used, such as title, subheadings, page numbers, page headers or footers, and bulleted lists.

Overall

Circle the trait you used most effectively in your expository piece.			
Ideas	Organization	Voice	Word Choice
Sentence Fluency	Conventions	Presentation	
Explain why:			

Circle the trait you used least effectively in your expository piece.			
Ideas	Organization	Voice	Word Choice
Sentence Fluency	Conventions	Presentation	
Explain why:			

What is your plan for improving upon the trait you feel needs the most work?

Persuasive Writing Conference Planner

Name _____ Class _____

Before our conference on your persuasive piece, read the list of questions and directions after the trait(s) that I've highlighted on this sheet. We'll review your responses in the conference.

Ideas

Finding a Topic: Restate your topic in a simple sentence.	Focusing the Topic: What is your position on this topic?

Developing the Topic: Circle the techniques you used to persuade the reader to accept your point of view.

statistics	quotes	examples	personal opinions	predictions	comparisons	well-known facts	little-known facts

Using Details: Circle at least three details in your piece that are particularly strong and will likely persuade the reader to accept your point of view.

Organization

Creating the Lead: Circle the type of lead you used in your persuasive piece.

analogy or comparison	anecdote or case history	direct address	fact
metaphor	description	one word/phrase	controversial statement
statistic	summary	other:	

Using Sequence Words and Transition Words: Underline the sequence words and phrases in your piece. Then, put a box around transition words or phrases.

Structuring the Body: How many sentences did you devote to your side of the argument? _____
How many to the other? _____ Make sure you have more sentences that support your side of the argument.

Ending With a Sense of Resolution: What image did you create or what point did you make at the end to nail your position?

Voice

Establishing a Tone: Name the tone(s) of your piece here.

Conveying the Purpose: Highlight a section that is particularly credible and convincing.

Creating a Connection to the Audience	
Name this piece's audience.	Put a check next to any words or phrases that you selected just for that audience.

Taking Risks to Create Voice: What did you do that might surprise the reader but that will help convince him or her that your side of the argument is stronger?

Word Choice

Applying Strong Verbs: Circle your three strongest verbs.

Selecting Striking Words and Phrases: Star your most visual word or phrase.

Using Specific and Accurate Words: Put a box around the words and phrases you revised to make them more specific or accurate.

Choosing Words That Deepen Meaning: Underline the word or phrase that you believe captures the essence of your argument.

Sentence Fluency

Crafting Well-Built Sentences: Check your sentences to make sure the subjects vary from sentence to sentence. Underline any that should be revised because their construction is too repetitive.

Varying Sentence Types: Label each of your simple sentences with a 1, compound sentences with a 2, complex sentences with a 3, and compound-complex sentences with a 4. Put a star by the type of sentence you used most often.

Capturing Smooth and Rhythmic Flow: Read your piece aloud to a partner. Put a check by any section that needs to be smoothed out.

Breaking the "Rules" to Create Fluency: Highlight any examples in which you broke rules to create fluency in your piece, such as by using a fragment.

Conventions

Checking Spelling: List three words you feel are a stretch for you to spell.

Punctuating Effectively and Paragraphing Accurately: Highlight an example of how you used punctuation to help your reader engage with a key point. Highlight an example of how you used paragraphing accurately.

Capitalizing Correctly: Double-check all proper nouns and sentence beginnings for capitalization. Circle the words in your title that are capitalized correctly.

Applying Grammar and Usage: Make sure your subjects and verbs agree. Underline an example. Do your pronouns and antecedents match? Underline an example.

Presentation

Applying Handwriting Skills: Highlight the section that is easiest to read. Underline the section that would most benefit from better handwriting.

Using Word Processing Effectively: What font and size did you choose?

Is the font easy to read?	Is it appropriate for your audience?

Making Good Use of White Space: Make sure your margins neatly frame the text. Did you leave room around the edges? Did you double-space the text, if requested?

Refining Text Features: List text features you used, such as title, subheadings, page numbers, page headers or footers, and bulleted lists.

Overall

Circle the trait you used most effectively in your persuasive piece.			
Ideas	Organization	Voice	Word Choice
Sentence Fluency	Conventions	Presentation	
Explain why:			

Circle the trait you used least effectively in your persuasive piece.			
Ideas	Organization	Voice	Word Choice
Sentence Fluency	Conventions	Presentation	
Explain why:			

What is your plan for improving upon the trait you feel needs the most work?

Home Communication Forms

Middle schoolers can get support in writing at home as well as at school. The forms in this section are designed to give parents and other significant adults in the student's life information they need in order to be good readers of and responders to students' work by focusing on specific traits and modes. As a result, students learn how their writing comes across to an audience other than the teacher.

SEE PAGE 49

Sample Teacher-to-Home Letter

This letter explains to parents and caregivers what the traits are and how to help student writers apply them wisely. Whether you sign, photocopy, and send it home as is, or adapt it to meet your individual goals, the letter paves the way to open communication about writing between home and school early in the school year.

Trait Writer-to-Reader Letters

The trait writer-to-reader letters invite parents and caregivers to interact with the student about his or her writing. As you work on each trait, make photocopies of the appropriate letter, distribute it to students, and have students attach the letter to their writing. At home, students should read their work aloud to a trusted adult and ask the questions in the letter. The answers always spur good dialogue, as well as ideas for editing and revision. Sending these letters home on a regular basis will help family members become more skilled at encouraging improvements.

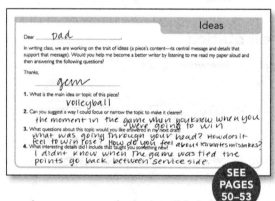

SEE PAGES 50–53

Mode Writer-to-Reader Letters

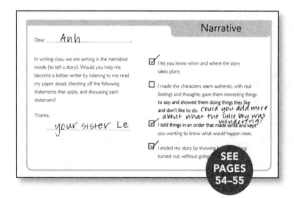

SEE PAGES 54–55

The mode writer-to-reader letters define the writing modes (narrative, expository, and persuasive) for parents and other caregivers who help the student with his or her writing. As you work on each mode, make photocopies of the appropriate letter, distribute it to students, and have students attach the letter to their writing. Each letter encourages the student to read his or her work aloud and then have a trusted adult fill in the quick checklist. Writers and readers then discuss each checklist statement, which always inspires ideas for revision. Sending these letters home on a regular basis will help family members become more skilled at encouraging improvement in the various writing modes.

Dear _____ :

Welcome to the exciting world of middle school writing using the traits, an assessment model that guides my instruction as I teach students the seven qualities of good writing.

* **Interesting ideas:** The piece's content—its central message and details that support that message.

* **Logical organization:** The internal structure of the piece—the thread of logic, the pattern of meaning.

* **Purposeful voice:** The tone and tenor of the piece—the personal stamp of the writer, which is achieved through a strong understanding of purpose and audience.

* **Precise word choice:** The specific vocabulary the writer uses to convey meaning and enlighten the reader.

* **Smooth sentence fluency:** The way words and phrases flow through the piece. It is the auditory trait because it is "read" with the ear as much as the eye.

* **Accurate conventions:** The mechanical correctness of the piece. Correct use of conventions (spelling, capitalization, punctuation, paragraphing, and grammar and usage) guides the reader through the text and makes it easy to follow.

* **Attractive presentation:** The physical appearance of the piece. A visually appealing text provides a welcome mat. It invites the reader in.

During the year, middle school students will learn how to apply these traits to their work to create strong and powerful writing for many purposes and audiences. As we are learning, however, don't be too concerned if papers come home that are not marked for spelling or other conventions. Rest assured that we will be working on this important trait; however, sometimes we may focus our attention on one or more of the other traits as well. Your middle school writer will learn a great deal about writing this year!

As we tackle each of these traits, I'd like to request your help. Periodically, your student writer will come home with Trait Writer-to-Reader Letters that contain questions about his or her writing. Please listen as the piece is read aloud and then answer and discuss the questions in the letter. It's that simple. By providing a good listening ear and constructive feedback, you can play a crucial role in your child's writing success. Thank you in advance for your help and support. I welcome your comments and suggestions as our writing program kicks into gear.

Sincerely,

Trait Writer-to-Reader Letters

Ideas

Dear _____,

In writing class, we are working on the trait of ideas (a piece's content—its central message and details that support that message). Would you help me become a better writer by listening to me read my paper aloud and then answering the following questions?

Thanks,

_____

1. What is the main idea or topic of this piece?

2. Can you suggest a way I could focus or narrow the topic to make it clearer?

3. What questions about this topic would you like answered in my next draft?

4. What interesting details did I include that taught you something new?

Organization

Dear _____,

In writing class, we are working on the trait of organization (the internal structure of a piece). Would you help me become a better writer by listening to me read my paper aloud and then answering the following questions?

Thanks,

_____

1. Did my lead capture your interest and make you want to keep listening?

2. Will you please point out any sequence or transition words and phrases that show connections between sentences or paragraphs, such as *finally* and *however*?

3. Were there places in my writing where I should have sped up or slowed down?

4. Did I give you something interesting to think about at the end? If so, what?

Voice

Dear _____,

In writing class, we are working on the trait of voice (the tone and tenor of a piece—the personal stamp of the writer, which is achieved through a strong understanding of purpose and audience). Would you help me become a better writer by listening to me read my paper aloud and then answering the following questions?

Thanks,

_____

1. Can you name the tone of the writing (happy, sad, thoughtful, wise, and so on)?

2. Is this the right tone for the piece?

3. Do you understand what I think and feel about my topic?

4. Is my writing interesting, fresh, and original? Show me where in particular.

Word Choice

Dear _____,

In writing class, we are working on the trait of word choice (the specific vocabulary a writer uses to convey meaning and enlighten the reader). Would you help me become a better writer by listening to me read my paper aloud and then answering the following questions?

Thanks,

_____

1. Did I use action words—or strong verbs? Tell me a few that you heard.

2. Do you think I used the right words in just the right places? If so, where? If not, where should I have?

3. Do any words or phrases confuse you?

4. What is your favorite word or phrase?

Trait Writer-to-Reader Letters

Sentence Fluency

Dear _____,

In writing class, we are working on the trait of sentence fluency (the way words and phrases flow through a piece). Would you help me become a better writer by listening to me read my paper aloud and then answering the following questions?

Thanks,

_____

1. Did I vary the beginnings and lengths of my sentences to add energy?

2. Did I use different types of sentences?

3. Do you think the writing contains a smooth flow of words and phrases? Was it easy for you to listen to me read it aloud?

4. Can you identify a sentence in my writing in which I tried something challenging or surprising?

Conventions

Dear _____,

In writing class, we are working on the trait of conventions (spelling, punctuation, paragraphing, capitalization, and grammar and usage). Would you help me become a better writer by following along as I read my paper aloud and then answering the following questions?

Thanks,

_____

1. Did you find any spelling mistakes?

2. Is my punctuation correct? How about my paragraphs?

3. Did I capitalize in all the right places?

4. Does my grammar and usage follow the rules of standard English?

Presentation

Dear _____,

In writing class, we are working on the trait of presentation (the physical appearance of a piece). Would you help me become a better writer by following along as I read my paper aloud and then answering the following questions?

Thanks,

_____

1. Is my handwriting easy to read?

2. If I used a word processor to create the piece, is my choice of font style and size consistent and appropriate?

3. Does the page's white space allow you to focus on the text, or is it distracting?

4. Have I successfully used headers, page numbers, graphics, or bullets to make it easy to find information? Have I effectively integrated any charts, graphs, maps, tables, or illustrations into the text?

Traits of Writing

Dear _____,

In writing class, we are working on all of the traits of writing. Would you help me become a better writer by following along as I read my paper aloud and then answering the following questions?

Thanks,

_____

1. Which trait(s) have I applied best in this paper?

Ideas	Organization	Voice	Word Choice
Sentence Fluency	Conventions	Presentation	

2. If I could work on one trait to improve this piece of writing, which one should it be?

3. If you could rate this paper on a scale of 1 to 6, what score would you give it?

1	2	3	4	5	6
Getting Started	On Your Way	Making Strides	Almost There	Well Done	Expert

4. Where do you think my writing shows the most improvement?

Mode Writer-to-Reader Letters

Narrative

Dear _____,

In writing class, we are writing in the narrative mode (to tell a story). Would you help me become a better writer by listening to me read my paper aloud, checking off the following statements that apply, and discussing each statement?

Thanks,

_____

- ☐ I let you know when and where the story takes place.

- ☐ I made the characters seem authentic, with real feelings and thoughts; gave them interesting things to say; and showed them doing things they like and don't like to do.

- ☐ I told things in an order that made sense and kept you wanting to know what would happen next.

- ☐ I ended my story by showing how everything turned out, without going on for too long.

Expository

Dear _____,

In writing class, we are writing in the expository mode (to inform or explain). Would you help me become a better writer by listening to me read my paper aloud, checking off the following statements that apply, and discussing each statement?

Thanks,

_____

- ☐ I provided information about something you didn't already know.

- ☐ I used creative, interesting details and examples to support my topic.

- ☐ I thought of questions you might ask and tried to answer them.

- ☐ I made all the information as clear and easy to understand as possible.

Persuasive

Dear _____,

In writing class, we are writing in the persuasive mode (to construct an argument). Would you help me become a better writer by listening to me read my paper aloud, checking off the following statements that apply, and discussing each statement?

Thanks,

_____

☐ I chose a topic and stuck with it throughout the piece.

☐ I made my position on that topic crystal clear to you.

☐ I provided you with good, sound, well-supported reasons for agreeing with my position.

☐ I considered the other side of the argument and explained its weaknesses convincingly.

SECTION 2

Reproducible Forms for Students

I n this section, you'll find two sets of forms that students can use to help them at each step in the writing process and to monitor their own progress in writing:

* Forms for Drafting, Revising, and Editing

* Self-Assessment Tools

Students who apply the traits on a systematic, ongoing basis develop insight into what makes writing work. They develop skills in drafting, revising, and editing—three cornerstones of the writing process—and they get an insider's perspective on what to do to improve writing over time. These are useful skills that are based, in part, on an understanding of the traits.

Furthermore, students thrive when they are given the tools to measure their own progress and see firsthand what they are doing well and what needs improvement. It's motivating and encouraging—two keys to success. That's why self-assessment is so important.

The forms that follow are designed to make your work with students easier and more purposeful. As students gain appreciation for how the writing traits and the writing process work together, and build the skills to pause and reflect on their own work, they take big steps toward becoming self-motivated, self-confident, lifelong writers.

Forms for Drafting, Revising, and Editing

Think of the traits not only as an assessment tool but also as an instructional tool for helping students learn to revise and edit—two powerful steps in the writing process. The first five traits—ideas, organization, voice, word choice, and sentence fluency—are the revision traits. These traits are applied to make writing as clear as possible. The last two traits, conventions and presentation, are what writers consider when they edit—or when they prepare their work for the reader—using commonly accepted rules of English language. Students who learn the difference between revision and editing, and how the traits fit within them, have inside knowledge on the writing process, which will be useful to them for the rest of their writing lives.

Key Qualities of the Revision and Editing Traits

There are seven traits for students to learn and apply to their writing. Within those traits, there is much to be learned. Over time, teachers have come to understand that even though the traits break the writing down into smaller, more manageable parts, each trait covers a lot of territory—often too much to teach effectively. That's why the new version of the scoring guides on pages 12–18 breaks down each trait into four key qualities that explain the characteristics of the trait. The key qualities also provide 28 essential revision and editing skills to teach throughout the year, which is quite achievable. Use these reproducible lists of key qualities to help students remember each trait's key qualities as you teach them throughout the year.

"Think Abouts" for Each Trait's Key Qualities

Whereas the key qualities help you and your students understand the different characteristics of each trait, the four Think About questions for each key quality are designed to stimulate thinking as students draft, revise, and edit. Use the seven Think About forms to help students gain a better understanding of each trait and its key qualities. These forms encourage students to ask themselves important questions about each trait as they focus on it in writing. Also, when students work with partners, the forms can prompt specific questions about each others' work.

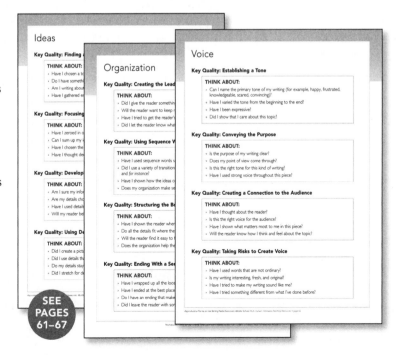

SEE PAGES 59–60

SEE PAGES 61–67

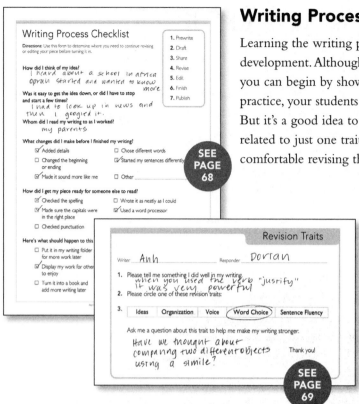

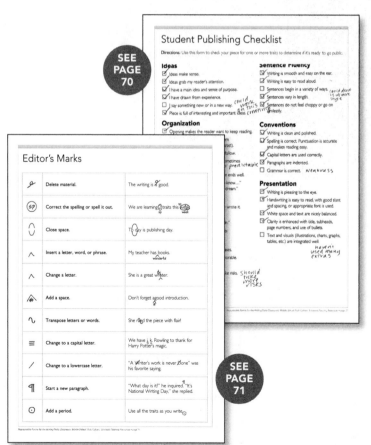

Writing Process Checklist

Learning the writing process is an important step in every writer's development. Although revision may be the area students resist the most, you can begin by showing students the possibilities with this form. With practice, your students will be able to complete all the steps on this form. But it's a good idea to start with one question and focus on the skills related to just one trait. Move on from there as students become more comfortable revising their work over time.

Peer Conference Guides

Students can help each other with revision and editing by following the steps on the two peer conference guides. Photocopy both guides and ask students to select the one that matches the trait they will talk about with their partner during writing workshop. The guide will provide structure for the peer conference.

Student Publishing Checklist

This is a versatile checklist that can be used in its entirety to check whether a paper is ready for a final copy, or used in sections for revision and editing, one trait at a time. Written in student-friendly language, it allows middle school writers to home in on strengths and weaknesses without overwhelming them with too much information. This form is also useful for peer feedback.

Editor's Marks

This handy reference sheet acquaints student writers with common editor's marks. Photocopy enough for the class and encourage students to use the sheets when they're editing their papers for style and accuracy. If you like, you can enlarge this form to poster size and hang it in a prominent place for everyone to refer to as they write.

Key Qualities of the Revision Traits

Ideas
* Finding a Topic
* Focusing the Topic
* Developing the Topic
* Using Details

Organization
* Creating the Lead
* Using Sequence Words and Transition Words
* Structuring the Body
* Ending With a Sense of Resolution

Voice
* Establishing a Tone
* Conveying the Purpose
* Creating a Connection to the Audience
* Taking Risks to Create Voice

Word Choice
* Applying Strong Verbs
* Selecting Striking Words and Phrases
* Using Specific and Accurate Words
* Choosing Words That Deepen Meaning

Sentence Fluency
* Crafting Well-Built Sentences
* Varying Sentence Types
* Capturing Smooth and Rhythmic Flow
* Breaking the "Rules" to Create Fluency

Key Qualities of the Editing Traits

Conventions

 * Checking Spelling

 * Punctuating Effectively and Paragraphing Accurately

 * Capitalizing Correctly

 * Applying Grammar and Usage

Presentation

 * Applying Handwriting Skills

 * Using Word Processing Effectively

 * Making Good Use of White Space

 * Refining Text Features

Ideas

Key Quality: Finding a Topic

THINK ABOUT:

- Have I chosen a topic that I really like?
- Do I have something new to say about this topic?
- Am I writing about what I know and care about?
- Have I gathered enough information about it so that I'm ready to write?

Key Quality: Focusing the Topic

THINK ABOUT:

- Have I zeroed in on one small part of a bigger idea?
- Can I sum up my idea in a simple sentence?
- Have I chosen the information that captures my idea best?
- Have I thought deeply about what the reader will need to know?

Key Quality: Developing the Topic

THINK ABOUT:

- Am I sure my information is right?
- Are my details chock-full of interesting information?
- Have I used details that show new thinking about this idea?
- Will my reader believe what I say about this topic?

Key Quality: Using Details

THINK ABOUT:

- Did I create a picture in the reader's mind?
- Did I use details that draw upon the five senses (sight, touch, taste, smell, hearing)?
- Do my details stay on the main topic?
- Did I stretch for details beyond the obvious?

Organization

Key Quality: Creating the Lead

THINK ABOUT:

- Did I give the reader something interesting to think about right from the start?
- Will the reader want to keep reading?
- Have I tried to get the reader's attention?
- Did I let the reader know what is coming?

Key Quality: Using Sequence Words and Transition Words

THINK ABOUT:

- Have I used sequence words such as *later*, *then*, and *meanwhile*?
- Did I use a variety of transition words such as *however*, *because*, *also*, and *for instance*?
- Have I shown how the ideas connect from sentence to sentence?
- Does my organization make sense from paragraph to paragraph?

Key Quality: Structuring the Body

THINK ABOUT:

- Have I shown the reader where to slow down and where to speed up?
- Do all the details fit where they are placed?
- Will the reader find it easy to follow my ideas?
- Does the organization help the main idea stand out?

Key Quality: Ending With a Sense of Resolution

THINK ABOUT:

- Have I wrapped up all the loose ends?
- Have I ended at the best place?
- Do I have an ending that makes my writing feel finished?
- Did I leave the reader with something to think about?

Voice

Key Quality: Establishing a Tone

THINK ABOUT:

- Can I name the primary tone of my writing (for example, happy, frustrated, knowledgeable, scared, convincing)?
- Have I varied the tone from the beginning to the end?
- Have I been expressive?
- Did I show that I care about this topic?

Key Quality: Conveying the Purpose

THINK ABOUT:

- Is the purpose of my writing clear?
- Does my point of view come through?
- Is this the right tone for this kind of writing?
- Have I used strong voice throughout this piece?

Key Quality: Creating a Connection to the Audience

THINK ABOUT:

- Have I thought about the reader?
- Is this the right voice for the audience?
- Have I shown what matters most to me in this piece?
- Will the reader know how I think and feel about the topic?

Key Quality: Taking Risks to Create Voice

THINK ABOUT:

- Have I used words that are not ordinary?
- Is my writing interesting, fresh, and original?
- Have I tried to make my writing sound like me?
- Have I tried something different from what I've done before?

Word Choice

Key Quality: Applying Strong Verbs

THINK ABOUT:

- Have I used action words?
- Did I stretch to get a better word—*scurry* rather than *run*?
- Do my verbs give my writing punch and pizzazz?
- Did I avoid *is, am, are, was, were, be, being,* and *been* whenever I could?

Key Quality: Selecting Striking Words and Phrases

THINK ABOUT:

- Did I try to use words that sound *just right*?
- Did I try hyphenating several shorter words to make an interesting-sounding new word?
- Did I try putting words with the same sound together?
- Did I read my piece aloud to find at least one or two moments I love?

Key Quality: Using Specific and Accurate Words

THINK ABOUT:

- Have I used nouns and modifiers that help the reader see a picture?
- Did I avoid using words that might confuse the reader?
- Did I try a new word and, if so, check to make sure I used it correctly?
- Are these the best words that can be used?

Key Quality: Choosing Words That Deepen Meaning

THINK ABOUT:

- Did I choose words that show I really thought about them?
- Have I tried to use words without repeating myself?
- Do my words capture the reader's imagination?
- Have I found the best way to express myself?

Sentence Fluency

Key Quality: Crafting Well-Built Sentences

THINK ABOUT:

- Do my sentences begin in different ways?
- Are my sentences of different lengths?
- Are my sentences grammatically correct unless constructed creatively for impact?
- Have I used conjunctions such as *but*, *and*, and *so* to connect parts of sentences?

Key Quality: Varying Sentence Types

THINK ABOUT:

- Do I include different kinds of sentences?
- Are some of my sentences complex?
- Are some of my sentences simple?
- Did I intermingle sentence types, one to the next?

Key Quality: Capturing Smooth and Rhythmic Flow

THINK ABOUT:

- Is reading the entire piece aloud easy?
- Do my sentences flow, one to the next?
- Do individual passages sound smooth when I read them aloud?
- Did I thoughtfully place different sentence types to enhance the main idea?

Key Quality: Breaking the "Rules" to Create Fluency

THINK ABOUT:

- Did I use fragments with style and purpose?
- Do I begin a sentence informally to create a conversational tone?
- Does my dialogue sound authentic?
- Did I try weaving in exclamations and single words to add emphasis?

Conventions

Key Quality: Checking Spelling

THINK ABOUT:

- Have I used standard English spelling unless I chose not to for a good reason?
- Have I checked words with *ie* and *ei*?
- When adding suffixes to words, have I changed *y* to *i*, doubled the final consonant, or dropped the silent *e* when necessary?
- Have I checked my work for words I have trouble spelling?

Key Quality: Punctuating Effectively and Paragraphing Accurately

THINK ABOUT:

- Did I place quotation marks around dialogue and direct quotes?
- Did I punctuate complex sentences correctly?
- Did I use apostrophes to show possessives and contractions?
- Did I begin new paragraphs in the appropriate places?

Key Quality: Capitalizing Correctly

THINK ABOUT:

- Did I capitalize proper nouns for people, places, and things?
- Did I capitalize dialogue correctly?
- Did I capitalize abbreviations, acronyms, and people's titles correctly?
- Did I capitalize the title and/or other headings?

Key Quality: Applying Grammar and Usage

THINK ABOUT:

- Did I correctly use special words such as homophones, synonyms, and antonyms?
- Did I check my sentences for subject-verb agreement?
- Did I use verb tense (past, present, future) consistently throughout my piece?
- Did I make sure pronouns and their antecedents (the words they stand for) agree?

Presentation

Key Quality: Applying Handwriting Skills

THINK ABOUT:

- Is my handwriting neat and legible?
- Did I take time to form each letter clearly?
- Do my letters slant in the same direction throughout?
- Does my spacing between words enhance readability?

Key Quality: Using Word Processing Effectively

THINK ABOUT:

- Is my choice of font style easy to read and appropriate for the audience?
- Is the font size appropriate?
- Did I effectively use formatting such as boldfacing, underlining, and italicizing?
- Does color enhance the look and feel of my piece—or does it weaken them?

Key Quality: Making Good Use of White Space

THINK ABOUT:

- Do my margins frame the text evenly on all four sides?
- Did I leave enough white space between letters, words, and lines to make the piece easy to read?
- Did I avoid cross-outs, smudges, and tears?
- Did I create a nice balance of text, text features, illustrations, photographs, and white space?

Key Quality: Refining Text Features

THINK ABOUT:

- Do my illustrations and photographs help make the piece easy to understand?
- Did I include my name, date, title, page numbers, and headers and footers?
- Are text features such as bulleted lists, sidebars, and timelines clear, well positioned, and effective in guiding the reader and enhancing meaning?
- Are charts, graphs, and tables easy to read and understand?

Writing Process Checklist

Directions: Use this form to determine where you need to continue revising or editing your piece before turning it in.

1. Prewrite
2. Draft
3. Share
4. Revise
5. Edit
6. Finish
7. Publish

How did I think of my idea?

Was it easy to get the idea down, or did I have to stop and start a few times?

Whom did I read my writing to as I worked?

What changes did I make before I finished my writing?

- ☐ Added details
- ☐ Changed the beginning or ending
- ☐ Made it sound more like me

- ☐ Chose different words
- ☐ Started my sentences differently
- ☐ Other _____

How did I get my piece ready for someone else to read?

- ☐ Checked the spelling
- ☐ Made sure the capitals were in the right place
- ☐ Checked punctuation

- ☐ Wrote it as neatly as I could
- ☐ Used a word processor

Here's what should happen to this paper next:

- ☐ Put it in my writing folder for more work later
- ☐ Display my work for others to enjoy
- ☐ Turn it into a book and add more writing later

- ☐ Take it home
- ☐ Read it to other classmates

Revision Traits

Writer _____   Responder _____

1. Please listen to me read my writing.

2. Please tell me something I did well in my writing.

3. Please circle one of these revision traits:

Ideas	Organization	Voice	Word Choice	Sentence Fluency

Ask me a question about this trait to help me make my writing stronger.

Thank you!

Editing Traits

Writer _____   Responder _____

1. Please look at my writing with me as I read it aloud.

2. Please tell me something I did well in my writing.

3. Please circle one of these editing issues for the conventions trait:

Spelling	Punctuation	Paragraphing	Capitalization	Grammar and Usage

Show me one thing I did well with this trait and one place I could make it stronger.

Give me a tip to make the presentation as strong as possible, too.

Thank you!

Student Publishing Checklist

Directions: Use this form to check your piece for one or more traits to determine if it's ready to go public.

Ideas

☐ Ideas make sense.

☐ Ideas grab my reader's attention.

☐ I have a main idea and sense of purpose.

☐ I have drawn from experience.

☐ I say something new or in a new way.

☐ Piece is full of interesting and important ideas.

Organization

☐ Opening makes the reader want to keep reading.

☐ Writing has logical order or pattern (problem-solution, compare-contrast).

☐ Story or main points are easy to follow.

☐ Reader is able to predict but is sometimes surprised.

☐ Loose ends are tied up. The piece ends well.

☐ Piece doesn't end with "Now you know…" or "Then I awoke, and it was all a dream."

Voice

☐ This sounds like someone I know wrote it.

☐ Writing has style and flavor.

☐ Piece reaches out and "pulls me in."

☐ Piece makes me feel a certain way.

Word Choice

☐ I use just the right words and phrases.

☐ After reading, words are still memorable.

☐ Words are accurately used.

☐ Words are chosen wisely, but I take risks.

☐ I know the language of the topic but don't try to impress.

☐ Simple language is used effectively.

Sentence Fluency

☐ Writing is smooth and easy on the ear.

☐ Writing is easy to read aloud.

☐ Sentences begin in a variety of ways.

☐ Sentences vary in length.

☐ Sentences do not feel choppy or go on aimlessly.

Conventions

☐ Writing is clean and polished.

☐ Spelling is correct. Punctuation is accurate and makes reading easy.

☐ Capital letters are used correctly.

☐ Paragraphs are indented.

☐ Grammar is correct.

Presentation

☐ Writing is pleasing to the eye.

☐ Handwriting is easy to read, with good slant and spacing, or appropriate font is used.

☐ White space and text are nicely balanced.

☐ Clarity is enhanced with title, subheads, page numbers, and use of bullets.

☐ Text and visuals (illustrations, charts, graphs, tables, etc.) are integrated well.

Editor's Marks

Mark	Meaning	Example
ℒ	Delete material.	The writing is ~~is~~ good.
(sp)	Correct the spelling or spell it out.	We are learning ②traits this ⟨weak⟩
⌒	Close space.	To⌒day is publishing day.
∧	Insert a letter, word, or phrase.	My teacher has books. ∧wonderful
∧	Change a letter.	She is a great wri∧ter.
⩑ (#)	Add a space.	Don't forget a⩑good introduction.
∿	Transpose letters or words.	She ra∿ed the piece with flair!
☰	Change to a capital letter.	We have j. k. Rowling to thank for Harry Potter's magic.
/	Change to a lowercase letter.	"A W/riter's work is never D/one" was his favorite saying.
¶	Start a new paragraph.	"What day is it?" he inquired. ¶"It's National Writing Day," she replied.
⊙	Add a period.	Use all the traits as you write⊙

Self-Assessment Tools

Middle school students are experienced writers. Although there is always more for them to learn, drawing upon what they have already learned in earlier grades and putting that knowledge to work will help them become more reflective thinkers and writers. The forms in this section are designed to help students look critically at their work and find places to revise and edit—on their own.

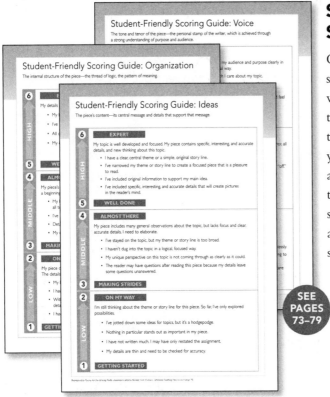

Student-Friendly Scoring Guides

Give students their own copies of the seven student-friendly scoring guides. As they write, point out the trait or traits you want them to focus on and ask them to assess their own writing before they share it with you. Students who don't see their writing as strong will need specific ideas on how to improve it, but the assessment is the first step along that path. Recognizing strengths and weaknesses in writing is an important skill all writers must master.

SEE PAGES 73–79

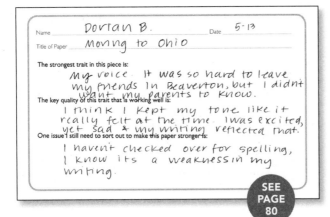

Self-Evaluation and Reflection Form

Use this form to spur students' thinking about what they have done well and what still needs work. As students learn to think about their writing, they will see a place for application of each of the traits. It's important to allow students time to reflect on what they have learned. By reviewing filled-out reflection forms, you also will gain valuable insights into what students know.

SEE PAGE 80

Student-Friendly Scoring Guide: Ideas

The piece's content—its central message and details that support that message.

---

6 HIGH

EXPERT

My topic is well developed and focused. My piece contains specific, interesting, and accurate details, and new thinking about this topic.

- I have a clear, central theme or a simple, original story line.
- I've narrowed my theme or story line to create a focused piece that is a pleasure to read.
- I've included original information to support my main idea.
- I've included specific, interesting, and accurate details that will create pictures in the reader's mind.

5 **WELL DONE**

---

4 MIDDLE

ALMOST THERE

My piece includes many general observations about the topic, but lacks focus and clear, accurate details. I need to elaborate.

- I've stayed on the topic, but my theme or story line is too broad.
- I haven't dug into the topic in a logical, focused way.
- My unique perspective on this topic is not coming through as clearly as it could.
- The reader may have questions after reading this piece because my details leave some questions unanswered.

3 **MAKING STRIDES**

---

2 LOW

ON MY WAY

I'm still thinking about the theme or story line for this piece. So far, I've only explored possibilities.

- I've jotted down some ideas for topics, but it's a hodgepodge.
- Nothing in particular stands out as important in my piece.
- I have not written much. I may have only restated the assignment.
- My details are thin and need to be checked for accuracy.

1 **GETTING STARTED**

Student-Friendly Scoring Guide: Organization

The internal structure of the piece—the thread of logic, the pattern of meaning.

6 HIGH

EXPERT

My details unfold in a logical order. The structure makes reading my piece a breeze.

- My beginning grabs the reader's attention.
- I've used sequence and transition words to guide the reader.
- All of my details fit together logically and move along smoothly.
- My ending gives the reader a sense of closure and something to think about.

5 WELL DONE

4 MIDDLE

ALMOST THERE

My piece's organization is pretty basic and predictable. I have the three essential ingredients, a beginning, middle, and end, but that's about it.

- My beginning is clear, but unoriginal. I've used a technique that writers use all too often.
- I've used simple sequence and transition words that stand out too much.
- Details need to be added or moved around to create a more logical flow of ideas.
- My ending needs work; it's pretty canned.

3 MAKING STRIDES

2 LOW

ON MY WAY

My piece doesn't make much sense because I haven't figured out a way to organize it. The details are jumbled together at this point.

- My beginning doesn't indicate where I'm going or why I'm going there.
- I have not grouped ideas or connected them using sequence and transition words.
- With no sense of order, it will be a challenge for the reader to sort out how the details relate.
- I haven't figured out how to end this piece.

1 GETTING STARTED

Student-Friendly Scoring Guide: Voice

The tone and tenor of the piece—the personal stamp of the writer, which is achieved through a strong understanding of purpose and audience.

HIGH

6
EXPERT

I've come up with my own "take" on the topic. I had my audience and purpose clearly in mind as I wrote and presented my ideas in an original way.

- My piece is expressive, which shows how much I care about my topic.
- The purpose for this piece is clear, and I've used a tone and tenor that are appropriate for that purpose.
- There is no doubt in my mind that the reader will understand how I think and feel about my topic.
- I've expressed myself in some new, original ways.

5
WELL DONE

MIDDLE

4
ALMOST THERE

My feelings about the topic come across as uninspired and predictable. The piece is not all that expressive, nor does it reveal a commitment to the topic.

- In a few places, my authentic voice comes through, but only in a few.
- My purpose for writing this piece is unclear to me, so the tone and tenor feel "off."
- I've made little effort to connect with the reader; I'm playing it safe.
- This piece sounds like lots of others on this topic. It's not very original.

3
MAKING STRIDES

LOW

2
ON MY WAY

I haven't thought at all about my purpose or audience for the piece and, therefore, my voice falls flat. I'm pretty indifferent to the topic and it shows.

- I've put no energy into this piece.
- My purpose for writing this piece is a mystery to me, so I'm casting about aimlessly.
- Since my topic isn't interesting to me, chances are my piece won't be interesting to the reader. I haven't thought about my audience.
- I have taken no risks. There is no evidence that I find this topic interesting or care about it at all.

1
GETTING STARTED

Student-Friendly Scoring Guide: Word Choice

The specific vocabulary the writer uses to convey meaning and enlighten the reader.

6

HIGH

EXPERT

The words and phrases I've selected are accurate, specific, and natural sounding. My piece conveys precisely what I want to say because of my powerful vocabulary.

- My piece contains strong verbs that bring it alive.

- I stretched by using the perfect words and phrases to convey my ideas.

- I've used content words and phrases with accuracy and precision.

- I've picked the best words and phrases, not just the first ones that came to mind.

5

WELL DONE

4

MIDDLE

ALMOST THERE

My words and phrases make sense but aren't very accurate, specific, or natural sounding. The reader won't have trouble understanding them. However, he or she may find them uninspiring.

- I've used passive voice. I should rethink passages that contain passive voice and add "action words."

- I haven't come up with extraordinary ways to say ordinary things.

- My content words and phrases are accurate but general. I might have overused jargon. I need to choose more precise words.

- I need to revise this piece by replacing its weak words and phrases with strong ones.

3

MAKING STRIDES

2

LOW

ON MY WAY

My words and phrases are so unclear the reader may wind up more confused than entertained, informed, or persuaded. I need to expand my vocabulary to improve this piece.

- My verbs are not strong. Passive voice permeates this piece.

- I've used bland words and phrases throughout—or the same words and phrases over and over.

- My content words are neither specific nor accurate enough to make the meaning clear.

- My words and phrases are not working; they distract the reader rather than guide him or her.

1

GETTING STARTED

Student-Friendly Scoring Guide: Sentence Fluency

The way words and phrases flow through the piece. It is the auditory trait because it's "read" with the ear as much as the eye.

6

HIGH

EXPERT

My piece is strong because I've written a variety of well-built sentences. I've woven those sentences together to create a smooth-sounding piece.

- I've constructed and connected my sentences for maximum impact.

- I've varied my sentence lengths and types—short and long, simple and complex.

- When I read my piece aloud, it is pleasing to my ear.

- I've broken grammar rules intentionally at points to create impact and interest.

5

WELL DONE

4

MIDDLE

ALMOST THERE

Although my sentences lack variety or creativity, most of them are grammatically correct. Some of them are smooth, while others are choppy and awkward.

- I've written solid shorter sentences. Now I need to try some longer ones.

- I've created different kinds of sentences but the result is uneven.

- When I read my piece aloud, I stumble in a few places.

- Any sentences that break grammar rules are accidental and don't work well.

3

MAKING STRIDES

2

LOW

ON MY WAY

My sentences are choppy, incomplete, or rambling. I need to revise my piece extensively to make it more readable.

- Many of my sentences don't work because they're poorly constructed.

- I've used the same sentence lengths and types over and over again.

- When I read my piece aloud, I stumble in many places.

- If I've broken grammar rules, it's not for stylistic reasons. It's because I may not understand those rules.

1

GETTING STARTED

Student-Friendly Scoring Guide: Conventions

The mechanical correctness of the piece. Correct use of conventions (spelling, capitalization, punctuation, paragraphing, and grammar and usage) guides the reader through text easily.

6 HIGH

EXPERT

My piece proves I can use a range of conventions with skill and creativity. It is ready for its intended audience.

- My spelling is strong. I've spelled all or nearly all the words accurately.
- I've used punctuation creatively and correctly and begun new paragraphs in the right places.
- I've used capital letters correctly throughout my piece, even in tricky places.
- I've taken care to apply standard English grammar and usage.

5 ### WELL DONE

4 MIDDLE

ALMOST THERE

My writing still needs editing to correct problems in one or more conventions. I've stuck to the basics and haven't tried challenging conventions.

- I've misspelled words that I use all the time, as well as complex words that I don't use as often.
- My punctuation is basically strong. I should review it one more time. I indented some of the paragraphs, but not all of them.
- I've correctly used capital letters in obvious places (such as the word *I*), but not in others.
- Even though my grammar and usage are not 100 percent correct, my audience should be able to read my piece.

3 ### MAKING STRIDES

2 LOW

ON MY WAY

The problems I'm having in conventions make this piece challenging to read, even for me! I've got lots of work to do before it's ready for its intended audience.

- Extensive spelling errors make my piece difficult to read and understand.
- I haven't punctuated or paragraphed the piece well, which is necessary to guide the reader.
- My use of capital letters is so inconsistent it's distracting.
- I need to clean up the piece considerably in terms of grammar and usage.

1 ### GETTING STARTED

Student-Friendly Scoring Guide: Presentation

The physical appearance of the piece. A visually appealing text provides a welcome mat. It invites the reader in.

6 — **EXPERT**

My piece's appearance makes it easy to read and enjoy. I've taken care to ensure that it is pleasing to my reader's eye.

- I've written clearly and legibly. My letters, words, and the spaces between them are uniform.
- My choice of font style, size, and/or color makes my piece a breeze to read.
- My margins frame the text nicely. There are no tears, smudges, or cross-outs.
- Text features such as bulleted lists, charts, pictures, and headers are working well.

5 — **WELL DONE**

HIGH

4 — **ALMOST THERE**

My piece still looks like a draft. Many visual elements should be cleaned up and handled with more care.

- My handwriting is readable, but my letters and words and the spaces between them should be treated more consistently.
- My choice of font style, size, and/or color seems "off"—inappropriate for my intended audience.
- My margins are uneven. There are some tears, smudges, or cross-outs.
- I've handled simple text features well but am struggling with the more complex ones.

3 — **MAKING STRIDES**

MIDDLE

2 — **ON MY WAY**

My piece is almost unreadable because of its appearance. It's not ready for anyone but me to read.

- My handwriting is so hard to read it creates a visual barrier.
- The font styles, sizes, and/or colors I've chosen are dizzying. They're not working.
- My margins are uneven or nonexistent, making the piece difficult to read.
- I haven't used text features well, even simple ones.

1 — **GETTING STARTED**

LOW

Self-Evaluation and Reflection Form

Name _____ Date _____

Title of Paper _____

The strongest trait in this piece is:

The key quality of this trait that is working well is:

One issue I still need to sort out to make this paper stronger is:

Name _____ Date _____

Title of Paper _____

The strongest trait in this piece is:

The key quality of this trait that is working well is:

One issue I still need to sort out to make this paper stronger is: